WOMEN in the CIVIL WAR

Other Books by Penny Colman:

NONFICTION:

Breaking the Chains: The Crusade of Dorothea Lynde Dix
Betsy Ross: Nimble Fingers and Sharp Eyes
Fannie Lou Hamer: Fighting for the Vote
Madame C.J. Walker: I Have Built My Own Factory
Fifty Years Together, co-author with Stella Chess, M.D. and
 Alexander Thomas, M.D.
Grand Canyon Magic

FICTION:

Dark Closets and Noises in the Night
I Never Do Anything Bad

For Linda

ACKNOWLEDGMENTS

Special thanks go to the archivists who helped me uncover so much fascinating information about women Civil War spies. Judy Reynolds, Curator/Director of Warren Heritage Society, Front Royal, Virginia, provided a wealth of material about Belle Boyd. She also reviewed parts of this manuscript.

Thanks also go to Debra Bashman and Greg Carroll, West Virginia Division of Culture and History, Charleston, West Virginia; Jean Clackler, Elizabeth Stephenson Memorial Library, Summersville, West Virginia; Diane C. Cashman, Lower Cape Fear Historical Society, Wilmington, North Carolina; Willie Mae Shawver, Oakdale Cemetery, Wilmington, North Carolina; Corrine P. Hudgins, The Museum of the Confederacy, Richmond, Virginia; Teresa Roane, The Valentine Museum, Richmond, Virginia; Gwendolyn C. Wells, Richmond Newspapers, Inc.; Christine and Paul Carter, Harriet Tubman Home, Auburn, New York; and Hedy Leutner, Mahwah, New Jersey. Also thanks to Stephen Colman for carefully and thoughtfully reading the manuscript.

CONTENTS

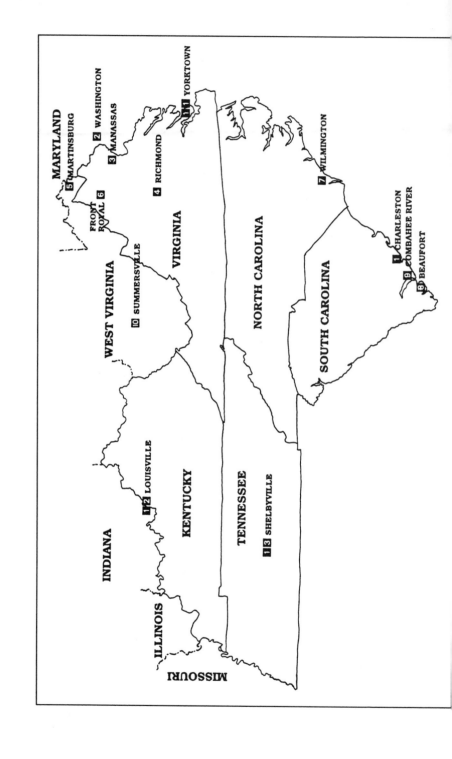

KEY TO MAP

1. CHARLESTON, SOUTH CAROLINA. Confederate troops opened fire on Union troops April 12, 1861.

2. WASHINGTON, D.C. Capital of the Union. Rose O'Neal Greenhow operated an extensive Confederate spy ring from her home here. Greenhow and Belle Boyd were imprisoned here in Old Capitol Prison.

3. MANASSAS, VIRGINIA. Located by Bull Run Creek and site of the first major land battle of the Civil War. Rose Greenhow provided indispensable information to the Confederates. Disguised as men, Sarah Emma Edmonds fought for the Union and Loreta Velazquez fought for the Confederacy in this battle.

4. RICHMOND, VIRGINIA. Capital of the Confederacy. Elizabeth Van Lew lived here and operated an extensive network of Union spies. Libby Prison was located here.

5. MARTINSBURG, WEST VIRGINIA. Belle Boyd lived here.

6. FRONT ROYAL, VIRGINIA. Belle Boyd's aunt and uncle lived here. This is where she made her famous dash across a battlefield to give military information to Confederate General Jackson.

7. WILMINGTON, NORTH CAROLINA. In May 1864, the steamer *Greyhound*, with Belle Boyd on board, tried to sail through the Union blockade. It was captured by a Union ship. In September, the steamer *Condor*, with Rose O'Neal Greenhow, arrived here from England. In an effort to avoid being captured by a Union ship, Greenhow drowned not far from shore.

8. BEAUFORT, SOUTH CAROLINA. Harriet Tubman sailed here on a ship from Boston, Massachusetts. She fought for the Union as a nurse, a scout, and a spy.

9. COMBAHEE RIVER, SOUTH CAROLINA. Harriet Tubman led three Union gunboats in a very successful raid up this river.

10. SUMMERSVILLE, WEST VIRGINIA. Nancy Hart was imprisoned by Union troops here. She killed her jailer, escaped, and returned with 200 Confederate soldiers to chase the Union soldiers away.

11. YORKTOWN, VIRGINIA. Sarah Emma Edmonds was stationed here. She disguised herself as a black laborer and spied behind Confederate lines nearby.

12. LOUISVILLE, KENTUCKY. Pauline Cushman tricked Confederate soldiers when she interrupted her theater performance to toast the Confederate president. In fact, she supported the Union and was a spy.

13. SHELBYVILLE, TENNESSEE. Pauline Cushman was arrested and sentenced to be hanged here. The day before she was to die, Union troops rescued her.

Chapter 1

WAR!

What awful times we have fallen upon!

The bloodiest, most devastating war fought on American soil—the Civil War—began on April 12, 1861. On a dark, cloudy morning, at 4:30 A.M. to be exact, Confederate troops in Charleston, South Carolina opened fire on the Union troops stationed in Fort Sumter. Thirty-four hours and about 3,500 shells later, Major Robert Anderson, the commander of Fort Sumter, surrendered.

News of the surrender reached President Abraham Lincoln in Washington, D.C. on April 14th. Determined to put down "the insurrection," Lincoln responded by issuing a proclamation calling for 75,000 volunteers. On the same day in New York City, Abby Howland Woolsey, who answered Lincoln's call by enlisting as a nurse, wrote a letter to her married sister, Elizabeth, in Fishkill, New York: "What awful times we have fallen upon!"

The awful times in the United States had been coming for a long time. And they revolved around the issue of slavery.

As early as 1619 the first Africans were brought to America and sold as slaves. As the country grew, so did the number of slaves. By 1860, four million black women, men, and children were enslaved in America. Mainly they worked in the tobacco and cotton fields located in the southern states of the United States—Mississippi, Alabama, South Carolina, Virginia, Georgia, and North Carolina.

Slavery never took hold in the Northern states such as New York, Pennsylvania, Massachusetts, and Maine, and most Northerners did not want slavery to spread. So, every time the United States gained new territory or a new state wanted to join the Union, Southerners and Northerners argued about the spread of slavery. There were also people called abolitionists who wanted to do more than stop the spread of slavery. They wanted to get rid of it. Everywhere. Forever.

For years Americans fought about slavery with words—speeches, newspaper articles, letters, and laws passed by Congress. These laws tried to satisfy both sides. In 1820, Congress allowed Missouri, part of the territory America got in the Louisiana Purchase of 1802, to enter the Union as a slave state. At the same time, it prohibited slavery in any other lands gained by the Louisiana Purchase, including the territories of Kansas and Nebraska. In 1850, Congress allowed California to enter the Union as a free state. At the same time, it toughened the Fugitive Slave Law that made it illegal to help runaway slaves.

But nothing satisfied either side for long. In 1854, the situation got worse when Congress passed the Kansas-Nebraska Act, which undid the law that had been passed in 1820. Now if the people in Kansas and Nebraska wanted slavery, they could have it. Congress could not stop them.

Finally, words weren't enough. With guns, fists, and lynching ropes, antislavery and proslavery people in Kansas and Nebraska fought for control. People in other parts of the country sent guns and money to the fighters. They argued about who was right and who was wrong. In Congress, proslavery Representative Preston Brooks of South Carolina used his cane to club anti-slavery Senator Charles Sumner of Massachusetts. "I wore out my cane completely," Brooks boasted as he proudly described his attack to reporters.

The turmoil continued.

14

In 1857, the Supreme Court ruled in the case of *Dred Scott* that slaves could never be citizens and that Congress had no right to limit the spread of slavery. Like a bolt of lightning, the *Dred Scott* decision jolted antislavery people into furious action. More and more Northerners declared themselves abolitionists. In Illinois, an antislavery lawyer named Abraham Lincoln decided to run for the Senate. A member of the Whig party, Lincoln switched to the newly formed Republican party because it was totally dedicated to stopping the spread of slavery.

Although Lincoln was defeated, his powerful speeches caught people's attention. In 1860, the Republicans selected Abraham Lincoln as their candidate for President. Winning every Northern state, Lincoln was elected President on November 6, 1860. In response, South Carolina seceded, or withdrew, from the Union. Then Mississippi, Florida, Alabama, Georgia, Louisiana, and Texas seceded and formed the Confederate States of America. Before long they were joined by Virginia, Tennessee, Arkansas, and North Carolina. Eleven Confederate states were pitted against twenty-three Union states.

The Union had more people, factories, railroads, and money, and a strong navy. The Confederacy had more military leaders. Before the war was over, millions of men would fight. More than a half a million would die—2,000 in one battle, 17,000 in another, and more than 50,000 dead at the Battle of Gettysburg. That is like killing most of the people who today live in American cities such as Santa Fe, New Mexico!

Millions of women would fight, too. They would fight as nurses, aides, and doctors on the battlefield, on hospital transport ships, and in field hospitals; as fundraisers and suppliers of money, clothing, bandages, and food; as workers in factories, in businesses, and on large and small farms; as soldiers disguised as men; and as spies.

Harriet Tubman was already a hero before the Civil War began because of her nineteen perilous trips south to rescue about 300 slaves. During the Civil War, she used her extraordinary courage and skills to fight for the Union as a nurse, scout, and spy. (Photo courtesy of J.B. Leib Photography Co., York, PA.)

Some women such as Sarah Emma Edmonds, who disguised herself as a man, played several roles—Union nurse, soldier, and spy. Other women such as Belle Boyd played just one role—Confederate spy. Women such as Dr. Mary Edwards Walker, a Union surgeon who was awarded the Medal of Honor for gallantry, were imprisoned. Women such as Loreta Janeta Velazquez, who disguised herself as a man and fought in several battles, were wounded. Women such as Mary A. Brady, a Union nurse who served heroically at the Battle of Gettysburg, died and were given funerals with full military honors.

As spies, women were particularly effective. The soldiers they helped were grateful. "Our President and our General direct me to thank you. We rely upon you for further information. The Confederacy owes you a debt," read the message from Major Thomas Jordan to Rose

O'Neal Greenhow after the Confederate victory at the Battle of Bull Run. "You have sent me the most valuable information received from Richmond during the war," General-in-Chief Ulysses Grant wrote in a message to Union spy Elizabeth Van Lew after his troops captured Richmond, the capital of the Confederacy.

Spying was a dangerous job. If caught, spies were treated like criminals and were often hanged—a most dishonorable and shameful fate. "I know there is no hope for mercy," condemned Union spy Timothy Webster wrote in a final request to his captor, "but, Sir, I beseech you to permit me to be shot, not be hanged like a common felon,—anything but that." His request refused, Webster was hanged. In fact, he was hanged twice, because the rope slipped and Webster fell to the ground the first time. As the guards returned him to the gallows, Timothy Webster said, "I suffer a double death."

Although there is no record of a woman spy being hanged, many were arrested. Others were imprisoned, some more than once. Pauline Cushman, a Union spy, was sentenced to hang. She was spared when her Confederate captors fled from a Union attack and left her behind.

A long list of women risked the dangers of spying. Some operated behind enemy lines and sent messages out with couriers. Others traveled back and forth themselves. Some used disguises. Union spy, scout, and commando Harriet Tubman disguised herself as a lame old woman. Elizabeth Van Lew dressed and acted so strangely that people dismissed her as "Crazy Bet." Mary Elizabeth Bowser, one of Van Lew's agents, worked as a servant on the staff of Jefferson Davis, the President of the Confederacy!

Disguised as a black laborer, Sarah Edmonds joined a work crew to learn about Confederate fortifications at Yorktown, Virginia. (The Union generals who sent her on the mission did not know she was a woman. She had fooled them with her disguise as a white male soldier, Franklin Thompson!)

On Edmonds' second day in the enemy camp, one of her fellow black workers gave her a puzzled look and said to his companion, "Jim, I'll be darned if that feller ain't turnin' white . . ." Making a joke about her mother being white, Edmonds slipped away to check her make-up. ". . . I took a look at my complexion by means of a small pocket looking-glass which I carried for that very purpose—and sure enough, as the negro had said, I was really turning white," Sarah Edmonds recalled later. "However, I had a small vial of nitrate of silver in weak solution, which I applied to prevent the remaining color from coming off."

Battles could be won or lost depending on the information spies provided. Accurate information about the enemies' plans and movements, their troop size and supplies, and the placement and strength of their fortification was indispensable. Spies could also intercept military dispatches or trick the enemy by spreading false information. A few generals did not completely trust spies—woman or man. But most did.

In fact, Union Major General Philip Sheridan actually recruited spies. In one case, he wrote a message on thin tissue paper, rolled it into a pellet, wrapped it in tin foil, and gave it to a black vegetable peddler to deliver to Rebecca Wright, a woman Sheridan hoped would help him. "I know from Major General Crook that you are a loyal lady and still love the old flag," Sheridan's message read. "Can you inform me of the position of Early's [a Confederate general] forces, the number of divisions in his army and the strength of any or all of them and his probable represented intentions? Have any troops arrived from Richmond, or any more coming?"

Hiding the pellet in his mouth, the peddler took it to Wright, a schoolteacher who lived in Winchester, Virginia—a town controlled by Early's troops. Despite great danger, Rebecca Wright obtained enough information to help Sheridan defeat Early and his army. In appreciation, Sheridan sent her a brooch and watch.

To keep information secret, many spies used codes by writing messages with words or phrases that actually stood for other words. "Tell Aunt Sally that I have some old shoes for the children ...," was the way Rose O'Neal Greenhow started one of her secret messages. In Greenhow's code, "old shoes" meant important information.

Spies also used ciphers in which different symbols were used to represent letters in the alphabet or other numbers. In the cipher Elizabeth Van Lew developed, the number 11 represented the letter "e" and the number 16 represented the number 3. Van Lew wrote the key to her cipher on a small piece of paper that she hid in the back of her watch.

Critical military information was sent in a variety of ways. An ordinary looking letter would carry a secret message written between the lines in invisible ink. Messages were written on onion skins and slipped into a slit in the sole of a courier's shoe. They were written on pieces of silk and sewn into a piece of clothing. Large metal buttons were also used as hiding places. Confederate spy Elizabeth Carraway Howland sent information in the hollow bone of a ham.

Another Confederate spy, known only as Mrs. M., wrapped around her dog's body a crucial report she had written. Then she sewed a fake coat of fur around the dog. Making her way through Union lines, Mrs. M. delivered herself and her dog to Confederate General Beauregard. "General, have you a knife about you?" she asked. The unsuspecting general handed her a knife, not realizing that she was going to cut open her dog! Beauregard was greatly relieved to see that the dog had more than one coat of fur.

Women's clothing—dresses with hoop skirts, long corsets, bonnets, and drawstring bags called reticules —were a spy's delight. All kinds of things were hung on the rings of steel wires that puffed out a hoop skirt—military maps, secret diagrams, bottles of medicine, guns, swords, and army boots. Why, a hoop skirt was full enough to hide a person; a strategy Confederate spy John Burke utilized on at least one occasion to avoid being captured. A women's corset, which extended from her hips to her breasts, was also a convenient hiding place.

Women hoped they would not be searched, and frequently they were not because it was a time when men prided themselves on being chivalrous. But as the war went on, women were searched more completely. According to Mary Chesnut, a prominent Southerner who kept detailed journals, "Women who come before the public are in a bad box now. False hair is taken off and searched for papers. Pistols are sought for ... Bustles are 'suspect.' All manner of things, they say, come over the border under the huge hoops now worn. So they are ruthlessly torn off. Not legs but arms are looked for under hoops."

Civil War women did not spy for fame or fortune. They spied because of their passionate convictions. Union spy Elizabeth Van Lew despised slavery. It "... crushes freedom of speech and of opinion ... is arrogant, is jealous and intrusive, is cruel, is despotic, not only over the slave but over the community, the state," Van Lew wrote in her diary. Confederate spy Belle Boyd was devoted to the South. Although in prison, Boyd told her jailer, "Sir, if it is a crime to love the South, its cause, and its President, then I am a criminal. I am in your power, do with me as you please. But I fear you not. I would rather lie down in this prison and die, then leave it owning allegiance to such a government as yours."

Women Civil War spies were smart, brave, committed, and clever. Their stories are awesome and inspiring. And in some cases, they are almost unbelievable!

Chapter 2

REBEL ROSE

*... I employed every capacity with which God has
endowed me.*

The South won the first major land battle of the Civil
War at Bull Run, or First Manassas as it is also remembered. Much of the credit was given to Confederate spy Rose O'Neal Greenhow. "Our President and our
General direct me to thank you. We rely on you for further information. The Confederacy owes you a debt,"
Colonel Thomas Jordan wrote to her shortly after the
battle. A year later, President Jefferson Davis had an
opportunity to tell her himself, "But for you there
would have been no Bull Run."

Brilliant, beautiful, and bold, Rose O'Neal Greenhow, a widow and mother of four children, was a powerful figure in Washington, D.C. James Buchanan, the
president before Abraham Lincoln, was her close
friend, as were leading senators, representatives, diplo-
mats, judges, and military leaders. The famous detective, Allan Pinkerton, described her as having "almost
irresistible seductive power." Union Colonel Erasmus
Keyes wrote that Greenhow was "the most persuasive
woman that was ever known in Washington." Dark-
eyed, dark-haired, olive-skinned, full figured, and witty,
Rose O'Neal Greenhow hosted elegant parties, private
meetings, and intimate conversations at her two-story
brick house on 16th Street, not far from the White
House and United States Capitol.

21

While they were prisoners, Rose O'Neal Greenhow and her daughter, Little Rose, had their photograph taken in the courtyard of Old Capitol Prison. Behind them is a window that has been covered over with wooden slats. (Photo courtesy of Lower Cape Fear Historical Society, Wilmington, North Carolina.)

Rose Greenhow paid close attention to political events. She went to Congress and listened to senators and representatives debate. She attended Supreme Court hearings. She read extensively. Well-traveled and fluent in several languages, Greenhow was articulate and confident. And she was unshakeable in her support of the South and the right of states to secede, or leave the United States. "I am a Southern woman, born with revolutionary blood in my veins," Greenhow wrote.

Although many people hoped that war could be avoided, Rose Greenhow thought it was inevitable. And she planned to be ready to serve the South. "I saw foreshadowed what was to follow," Greenhow wrote, "and I desired to obtain thorough insight into the plans and schemes of these who were destined to become the prominent actors in the fearful drama, in order that I might turn it to the advantage of my country when the hour for action arrived. "To this end I employed every capacity with which God has endowed me ..."

Colonel Thomas Jordan, a handsome man with a dark beard and firm look, was also preparing for war. Although he was a soldier in the United States Army, Jordan planned to resign and fight for the South. But before he did, he set about organizing a spy ring in Washington. The capital of the United States, Washington was the heart of the Union's political and military activity. It was also just across the Potomac River from Virginia and full of Southern sympathizers. What better place for a Confederate spy ring!

Well aware of Rose Greenhow's connections and ideals, Jordan approached her. He had a cipher. Would she be willing to send him information addressed to Thomas J. Rayford, an alias he had made up? Despite her grief over the recent death of her daughter, Gertrude, Rose O'Neal Greenhow agreed. Before long she was leading a large network of spies. It was a network that included dentists, professors, clerks, architects, servants, and cooks, and it reached as far as New Orleans and Boston, and across the ocean to London, Liverpool, and Paris.

Greenhow's connections and charm were not the only things that made her an effective spy. She also had keen eyes and ears, an extraordinary memory, and the ability to quickly comprehend the details — large and small — of military matters — fortifications, guns, ammunition, and soldiers. Her reports included maps, diagrams, and drawings. She also relayed her impressions and suggestions, such as: "Sickness and insubordination prevail more or less in all the regiments . . . Look out for batteries wherever you go . . . Their reliance this time is an abundance of artillery . . . an effort will be made here to cut their telegraph wires and if possible to spike their guns wherever they are left unmanned . . . A line of daily communication is now open . . . Send couriers . . ."

Despite her outspoken support of the South, Union officers and politicians continued to flock to Greenhow's house. Perhaps they thought she would not *dare* be a spy. Her own married daughter, Florence, and her husband, Treadwell Moore, did not even suspect she was a spy. Moore even wrote and asked his mother-in-law to use her connections to get him appointed a colonel in the Union army! And Florence wrote, "I am so much worried about the last news from Washington. They say some ladies have been taken up as spies ... Dear Mamma, do keep as clear of all Secessionists as you possibly can."

About three months after Fort Sumter surrendered, Rose O'Neal Greenhow received invaluable information. Union General Irvin McDowell planned to launch a surprise attack against General Beauregard and his 20,000 Confederate troops stationed at Manassas Junction near Bull Run Creek, about thirty miles from Washington. Then McDowell planned to march on to conquer Richmond, the Confederate Capital. Quickly Greenhow prepared a message to send to Jordan, who was now Beauregard's Adjutant-General. Her courier, Betty Duvall, disguised as a farm girl, set off to deliver it.

After safely crossing Union lines, Betty Duvall borrowed a horse from friends and dressed up as a fashionable lady out for a ride. Galloping off on her horse toward Manassas Junction, Duvall came upon Confederate General Milledge Bonham and his troops. Bonham never forgot their encounter. As he later wrote, Duvall was "a brunette, with sparkling black eyes, perfect features, glossy black hair ..."

Bonham assured Duvall that he would forward the message. So, as Bonham later recalled, "she took out her tucking comb and let fall the longest and most beautiful roll of hair I have ever seen. She took then from the back of her head, where it had been safely tied, a small package, not larger than a silver dollar, sewed up in silk."

Bonham forwarded the message. Without delay, Jordan sent a soldier, George Donellan, back to Greenhow for more information. (A month later, Donellan was in Richmond, where he visited the Chesnuts' house. "Found it quite exciting to have a spy drinking his tea with us," Mary Chesnut wrote in her diary. "Perhaps because I knew his profession, I did not like his face.")

Donellan arrived at Rose Greenhow's in the early morning hours. He told her that he had a message from Thomas J. Rayford, Jordan's alias. She read it. Written in Jordan's cipher, it said, "Trust Bearer."

Before long, Donellan left with another message from Greenhow hidden in the heel of one of his boots. He made his way back to Jordan by horse and buggy, boat, and horseback. The next day, he returned to Greenhow with a message from Jordan, "Yours was received at 8 o'clock at night. Let them come. We are ready for them. We rely upon you for precise information ..."

Greenhow's information prompted Beauregard to send a telegraph to Confederate President Jefferson Davis, "Send forward any reinforcements at the earliest possible instant and by every possible means." Without delay, Davis ordered General Joseph Johnston to get his troops there—fast.

On the 17th of July, Donellan brought a third message from Greenhow. New information had come to her about the Union's plan to cut the railroad lines, thus blocking Confederate reinforcements. Once again Rose Greenhow had gotten indispensable information.

Four days later, the main battle began. Ready and well-prepared, the Confederates routed the Union troops. Later Beauregard wrote that "he was almost as well informed of the strength of the hostile army in my front as its commander." The North was stunned; the South was jubilant. And, as mangled, dying, and dead soldiers were brought to Washington and Richmond, people on both sides got a look at the horror that had been unleashed.

Shortly after the battle at Bull Run, Jordan sent another message to Rose O'Neal Greenhow: "Our President and our General direct me to thank you. We rely upon you for further information. The Confederacy owes you a debt."

Greenhow continued spying; she gathered information about railroad operations, the defenses and fortifications around Washington, the comings and goings of troops, the number of rifles, and where hidden batteries were located. She knew about everything, including that there was a shortage of soldiers' blankets.

By August, Union officials became suspicious. It seemed that nothing could be kept secret, and it seemed that the leaks always led back to Rose O'Neal Greenhow. Union General George McClellan, who took over from McDowell after his defeat at Bull Run, said, "She knows my plans better than Lincoln or the Cabinet, and has four times compelled me to change them." Finally, Assistant Secretary of War, Thomas A. Scott, asked Allan Pinkerton, founder of a detective agency that is still functioning today, to watch Rose Greenhow.

In a book Pinkerton wrote after the war, he recalled his efforts to catch Rose Greenhow. "The entire day had been dark, gloomy and threatening . . .," Pinkerton wrote. "As I left my headquarters, a slight shower of rain was falling . . . Arriving at Mrs. Greenhow's, under cover of the darkness I posted my men as I thought would be most advantageous for our purposes . . ."

In an effort to see through the parlor windows, Pinkerton placed two of his men side by side, took off his boots, and climbed up on their shoulders. "I was now on a level with the windows, and noiselessly raising the sash and turning the slats of the blinds I obtained a full view of the interior of the room, but to my disappointment, it was unoccupied."

Suddenly one of Pinkerton's "sturdy supporters" warned him that someone was approaching. Scrambling for cover, Pinkerton and his men hid.

After the visitor entered, Pinkerton resumed his position at the window. He watched as Rose Greenhow greeted her visitor — a Union captain in full uniform whose "face lighted up with pleasure as he gazed upon her." Before long, Pinkerton saw the captain take a map out of his pocket and go over it with Greenhow. Then the "delectable couple disappeared."

Reappearing after more than an hour, Greenhow showed the captain to the door. Once again Pinkerton and his men hid under the stairs where they heard "a whispered good-night, and something that sounded very much like a kiss ..."

By then a rain storm was raging. That did not stop Pinkerton. He took off after the captain, and forgot to put his boots back on.

Unfortunately for Pinkerton, the Captain suspected he was being followed. As soon as he reached his headquarters he had "four armed soldiers" arrest Pinkerton. "I was a sorry sight to look at, and as I surveyed my weather-soaked and mud-stained garments, and my bare feet, I could scarcely repress a laugh, although I was deeply angered at the sudden and unexpected turn affairs had taken," Pinkerton recalled.

Pinkerton spent a miserable night in jail. He "shook like an aspen" and his "teeth chattered castanets." In the morning, he bribed a guard to inform Union officials that he was in jail. Pinkerton was quickly released. The Captain was arrested and imprisoned. Pinkerton returned to watch Rose O'Neal Greenhow.

Eight days later, on August 23, 1861, Allan Pinkerton approached Rose O'Neal Greenhow as she returned from a walk with a diplomat. Sensing danger, Greenhow quickly swallowed a ciphered message that she was carrying.

"I come to arrest you," Pinkerton said.

"I have no power to resist you," Greenhow replied, "but had I been inside of my house, I would have killed one of you before I had submitted to this illegal process."

Pinkerton took Greenhow into her house. Then he and his detectives conducted an extensive search, including Gertrude's room. Greenhow had left it undisturbed since Gertrude died.

According to Greenhow's account: "Men rushed

with frantic haste into my chamber, into every sanctuary. My beds, drawers, and wardrobes were all upturned; soiled clothes were pounced upon with avidity, and mercilessly exposed; papers that had not seen the light for years were dragged forth. My library was taken possession of, and every scrap of paper, every idle line was seized, even the torn fragments in the grates ..."

Boxes of evidence were carted away. (Modern readers can study them in the National Archives in Washington.) Fortunately for Greenhow, she was able to slip "papers of immense value" to her friend Lily Mackall, who smuggled them to safety in her boots.

Pinkerton kept Greenhow and little Rose, Greenhow's eight-year-old daughter, under house arrest for five months. At first he tried to keep her arrest a secret. He hoped to catch unsuspecting agents who stopped by. But he was foiled by little Rose, who ran into the garden, climbed a tree, and called out, "Mamma has been arrested. Mamma has been arrested."

Rose O'Neal Greenhow's house became quite the spot. Sightseers swarmed around while trying to glimpse the famous spy. Things got more interesting when Pinkerton decided to confine other women spies in Greenhow's house, or Greenhow Prison, as Rose Greenhow called it. It was also known as Fort Greenhow.

Despite her confinement, Rose O'Neal Greenhow managed to gather information and send messages. "Right under the eyes of my eighteen guards I received and answered dispatches from friends ...", she wrote. On one occasion, Greenhow smuggled out information wrapped in a ball of pink wool. Little Rose took the ball with her when she went for a walk with her guards. As she passed the house of sympathetic friends, Little Rose threw the yarn through their open window. "Here is the yarn you left at my house," she called out.

Pinkerton was totally frustrated. "She has not ceased to lay plans to attempt the bribery of officers having her in charge, to make signs from the windows of her house to her friends on the street ..." he reported.

Finally, on January 18, 1862, Rose O'Neal Greenhow was moved to Old Capitol Prison. Little Rose went with her. She was listed in the record book as "a dangerous, skillful spy." Ironically, the prison had once been her aunt's boarding house where Rose Greenhow had spent her teenage years. Now Greenhow and her daughter shared a room "about ten feet by twelve and furnished in the rudest manner—a straw bed with a pair of newly-made unbleached cotton sheets, a small feather pillow—a few wooden chairs, a wooden table and a glass [mirror] six by eight inches ... The windows were boarded up."

Prison did not stop Greenhow. With the flutter of her handkerchief, the shake of her head, the wiggle of her fingers, Rose Greenhow could receive and send messages. And although some of her agents had been arrested and many had fled, there were others. Her imprisonment caused quite a stir. Now the sightseers came to Old Capitol Prison. A guard told Greenhow that people would pay $10 just to see her.

In March, she had a hearing before the United States Commissioners for the Trial of State Prisoners. Although hollow-eyed and pale, Rose O'Neal Greenhow remained fiery. She refused to win her freedom by taking an oath of allegiance to the United States. And she refused to reveal any information about her activities. "I am a Southern woman, and I thank God that no drop of Yankee blood ever polluted my veins ..." she said.

Union officials were unable to change or silence Greenhow. They certainly could not hang her, because she still had powerful Union friends. Finally, they decided to send her to Richmond. So in June, she and little Rose left Old Capitol Prison. Concealed under her shawl, Rose O'Neal Greenhow carried a Confederate flag that she had made on her sewing machine, which a friendly guard had brought to Old Capitol Prison.

Confederate President Jefferson Davis visited Rose

O'Neal Greenhow when she arrived in Richmond. "Mrs. Greenhow is here," Davis wrote. "Madam looks much changed, and has the air of one whose nerves are shaken by mental torture."

It did not take Rose O'Neal Greenhow long to recover. Before the summer was over, she left on a secret mission to England and France. Little Rose went with her. Florence was waiting for them in England. (Her other daughter, Leile, was in a boarding school in Pennsylvania.) Her ship sailed from Wilmington, North Carolina, the safest port for Southern ships to run the Union blockade. "The Yankees are reported as being unusually vigilant, a double line of blockaders block the way," Greenhow reported in a letter to Jefferson Davis, "Still, I am nothing daunted and hope by the blessing of Providence, to get out in safety ..."

Union ships had been blocking—stopping and seizing—Confederate ships since the beginning of the war. At the time Greenhow sailed, one out of every seven Confederate ships was captured — a loss in supplies and ships that was a key to the South's ultimate defeat.

Rose Greenhow arrived safely in France. She had a private meeting with the Emperor of France, Napoleon III. She was formally presented at the French court. Traveling to England, she was presented to Queen Victoria. Everywhere Rose Greenhow went, she pleaded her cause. She wrote about her experiences in a book, *My Imprisonment and the First Year of Abolition Rule at Washington*. It was a great success.

Soon Greenhow was a celebrity. She thrived. Little Rose was happily settled in a convent school in Paris. She and her daughter Florence had put aside their political differences and become close again. Florence bought her clothes — a luxury Greenhow had not enjoyed since the war began. She enjoyed the company of important people—Florence Nightingale, the founder of modern nursing, Thomas Carlyle, the noted historian and philosopher, and Robert Browning, the famous poet. She also became engaged to marry Lord Granville.

But, before the wedding, Rose O'Neal Greenhow had to return to Richmond. She had not convinced the French and English governments to help the South. But she had bags full of important messages for Jefferson Davis, in addition to clothes for Southern women and gold that the Confederacy needed desperately — lots of gold, which was the profits from her book.

On August 10, 1864, Rose O'Neal Greenhow left England onboard the *Condor*, a new three-funnelled steamer. Exceptionally fast, the *Condor* was commanded by a legendary blockade runner who called himself Samuel S. Ridge. Not one to get seasick, Rose Greenhow loved to sail—the rocking and rolling motion, the spray from waves crashing over the sides. Other passengers noticed that Greenhow walked the deck even in the roughest weather. They also noticed that she always wore a large leather reticule, or drawstring bag, on a long chain around her neck. Little did they know that it was full of gold.

The *Condor* reached the waters off Wilmington, North Carolina on September 30, 1864. It was night, the best time to run the blockade. Not far from shore, the pilot accidentally ran the ship aground. Thrown from her bunk, Rose Greenhow got dressed and rushed on-deck. Suddenly someone spotted a Union ship close by! Were they in danger of capture? The captain did not think so, but Rose O'Neal Greenhow did not want to take the chance. She had to get to shore. She had to protect the bags of messages and the gold.

Greenhow asked the *Condor's* captain to send her ashore in a boat. He refused — it was much too dangerous—but she insisted. Back and forth Greenhow and the captain argued. Finally, Rose O'Neal Greenhow won.

Clutching her reticule, Greenhow climbed into an oar boat with five men—three crew men and two other Confederate agents who agreed to go with her. Almost as soon as they started out, a giant wave lifted the boat

Rose O'Neal Greenhow, a bold Confederate spy who ran a large spy ring in Washington, D.C. (Photo courtesy of J.B. Leib Photography Co., York, PA.)

up and over. The men hung onto the boat and were saved. But Rose O'Neal Greenhow had disappeared.

A Confederate soldier found Rose Greenhow's body washed ashore. The reticule was still around her neck. Opening it, the soldier found it full of gold. He stuffed it in his pockets and shoved Greenhow's body back into the ocean.

Her body washed ashore again. This time a search party found it. News of her death spread rapidly. People were stunned, including the soldier, who had not realized he had robbed the body of a Confederate hero. Overcome with guilt, the soldier confessed and returned the gold.

With an honor guard in attendance, Greenhow's body lay in state in Wilmington, North Carolina. Crowds gathered and shops closed for her funeral. She was buried with full military honors in Oakdale Cemetery, her coffin wrapped in a Confederate flag. Two inscriptions were chiseled on a plain marble cross. On the back were the words:

> Drowned off Fort Fisher, from the Steamer Condor, while attempting to run the blockade. Sept. 30, 1864.

And on the front was inscribed:

> Mrs. Rose O'N. Greenhow, a bearer of dispatches to the Confederate Government.

When the Capitol was destroyed by British troops during the War of 1812, this brick building was built across the street for temporary use by Congress. After the Capitol was rebuilt, this building became known as Old Capitol. Later Rose O'Neal Greenhow's aunt converted it into a boarding house. As a teenager, Rose lived there with her aunt. When the Civil War began, Union officials turned it into a prison. Called Old Capitol Prison, it was dilapidated and infested with lice and rats. Rose O'Neal Greenhow and her daughter, Little Rose, were imprisoned there. So was Belle Boyd. Eventually the Old Capitol building was torn down and replaced with the current U.S. Supreme Court Building. (Photo courtesy of J.B. Leib Photography Co., York, PA.)

Chapter 3

CRAZY BET

... my life was in continued jeopardy ...

The Union troops that Rose O'Neal Greenhow helped defeat at Bull Run had been on the way to capture Richmond, Virginia. Built along the James River and sprawling over seven hills, Richmond was the heart of the Confederacy. The city had stately houses along tree-lined streets, thriving businesses, huge tobacco warehouses, and the most important factory in the South—the Tredegar Iron Works. Confederate President Jefferson Davis lived there in the White House of the Confederacy.

Richmond was also a center of the slave trade. Many traders, agents, and auctioneers who bought and sold black women, men, and children were listed in the City Directory. And there were almost daily notices in the newspapers advertising the sale of slaves.

Over and over again Union generals tried to capture Richmond. First General McDowell, then McClellan, Burnside, Hooker, and Meade. Finally, General Ulysses S. Grant succeeded, four years after the Civil War began. After Grant captured Richmond, he had tea with one of the most successful spies for either side—Elizabeth Van Lew. "You have sent me the most valuable information received from Richmond during the war," Grant informed Van Lew.

Like Rose O'Neal Greenhow, Elizabeth Van Lew was in her early forties. She was a "pleasing, pale blond," according to one observer. Another person commented on the "almost unearthly brilliance" in her blue eyes. Her life-long friend, Mrs. E. Nowland, described her as "small but commanding ... a Napoleonic woman."

Van Lew wore her hair in dangling ringlets that softened her sharp features—thin lips, firm jaw, strong nose, and a high forehead. She was extraordinarily intelligent, clever, and courageous. According to Van Lew herself, she was "uncompromising, ready to resent what seemed wrong, quick and passionate but not bad tempered or vicious." And, according to a report written by General George Sharpe, Chief of the Bureau of Military Information, "For a long, long time, she represented all that was left of the power of the United States government in the city of Richmond."

Elizabeth Van Lew was a member of a prominent Richmond family. Although she was born and raised in Richmond, Van Lew's parents were originally Northerners. Her father was from New York. Her mother grew up in Philadelphia, Pennsylvania, where she was the daughter of Hillary Baker, a former mayor who heroically refused to leave his city during a yellow fever epidemic and died.

Elizabeth grew up with all the privileges of wealth. She lived in a magnificent mansion at the top of Church Hill, the highest hill in Richmond. Soaring three and one-half stories, the Van Lew mansion had stuccoed walls trimmed with limestone from Scotland. Matching semi-circular steps with iron balusters curved up on either side of a covered stone front porch with four pillars. A wide hallway ran straight through the mansion to a splendid portico, or covered porch, that ran the length of the huge house.

The view from the portico was spectacular — terraced gardens, live oak trees with Spanish moss hanging from the branches, magnolia trees with glossy leaves, boxwood hedges with tiny, shiny, dark green leaves that had a peculiar, musky odor, and, not far away, the

James River with its sparkling water and graceful curves. Gravel walks led through the gardens to a summer house and a moss-rimmed spring of cold, clear water. There was a barn for the Van Lews' four white matching horses and quarters for Mr. Van Lew's slaves.

The Van Lew mansion was at the center of Richmond's social life—garden parties, balls, formal dinners, dances, and intimate gatherings. John Marshall, chief justice of the Supreme Court and today known as the Great Chief Justice, was a frequent visitor. So was Edgar Allan Poe, the famous mystery writer. Jenny Lind, the famous Swedish soprano, during a tour of America sang in the Van Lews' parlor.

Elizabeth Van Lew was a gracious hostess. She was also outspoken. In particular, she was outspoken about slavery. After her parents sent her to school in Philadelphia—a center for abolitionists—she became fierce about it. When Fredrika Bremer, a renowned Swedish novelist, visited the Van Lews, she was drawn to Elizabeth because she "expressed so much compassion for the sufferings of the slave." Bremer wrote that after seeing slaves at work in a tobacco factory, "Good Miss Van L. could not refrain from weeping."

People in Richmond blamed Van Lew's attitudes on the Philadelphia abolitionists. But long before she went north to Philadelphia, Van Lew realized that she did not agree with most people in Richmond. "From the time I knew right from wrong it was my sad privilege to differ in many things from the . . . opinions and principles of my locality," she wrote.

Van Lew was twenty-five years old when her father died. Inheriting his slaves, she, her mother, and her brother, John, freed them. Several of the freed slaves decided to stay on as paid servants. One of them, Judy Johnson, became Van Lew's lifetime helper. Van Lew also bought and freed other slaves. She even sent Mary Elizabeth Bowser, another former Van Lew slave, to school in Philadelphia.

Elizabeth Van Lew, a brilliant Union spy in Richmond, Virginia, managed an extensive network of spies. (Photo courtesy of the Valentine Museum, Richmond, Virginia.)

Elizabeth Van Lew saw the first Confederate flag—the stars and bars—flying over Richmond on April 17, 1861. It was four days after the war began. That night she watched a torchlight parade in support of the Confederacy. She wept, and she committed herself to fight for the Union. "Never did a feeling of more calm determination and high resolve for endurance come over me," she wrote in her journal.

Van Lew had already been sending information to Washington. For two years before Fort Sumter surrendered, Van Lew had been writing letters to federal officials as she watched "the rise and spread of the secession mania." Now she sent information about the number, conditions, and movements of Confederate troops. Since the regular mail was no longer safe, Van Lew's servants agreed to be messengers.

With her mother, Van Lew watched the Confederate troops march off to fight the Union at Bull Run. Bands

38

played. Crowds cheered and threw flowers. A few days later, Richmonders were celebrating the South's victory. They were also coping with the horrors of war—soldiers wrapped in bloody bandages, arms and legs missing, blinded, dying soldiers and the dead. On July 21, 1861, Mary Chesnut wrote in her diary, "Today for the first time came a military funeral ... The empty saddle ... and the led war horse—we saw and heard it all ... it seems we are never out of the sound of the Dead March in *Saul* [music by George Frederick Handel that was used for military funerals]. It comes and it comes until I feel inclined to close my ears and scream."

There were also Union prisoners — hundreds of them. A warehouse was converted into a prison for captured officers. It was on the shore of the James River at the bottom of Van Lew's hill. Named Libby Prison after its owner, the warehouse was a grim place. Other prisoners such as foot soldiers were confined to tents on Belle Isle in the middle of the river and locked in miserable cells in Castle Thunder, known as a "Particular Hell."

Elizabeth Van Lew scurried around trying to get permission to nurse wounded Union soldiers. Finally she got a pass from General Winder, Provost-Marshall-General of Richmond, or the military commander of the city. Winder gave her "permission to visit the prisoners and to send them books, luxuries, delicacies, and what she may wish." Van Lew did all that and much more. She gathered invaluable information.

With whispered conversations and coded notes hidden in baskets of food, Van Lew let the prisoners know that she was a friend. She gave them books to read with significant words or numbers faintly underlined. The books might also have a message lightly penciled in between the lines or spelled out with tiny pin pricks. Soon the prisoners began to relay to her information they overheard from talkative prison guards and hospital doctors and nurses. They also observed much from their windows by watching the movement

The front of Elizabeth Van Lew's mansion, which stood at the top of Church Hill on Grace Street between 25th and 26th streets. Eleven years after Van Lew died, this beautiful and historic house was torn down. Today Richmond schoolchildren attend Bellevue School, which was built on the site. (Photo courtesy of the Valentine Museum, Richmond, Virginia.)

of Confederate troops and supplies.

Almost immediately, people tried to stop Van Lew's prison visits. A newspaper article attacked Van Lew and her mother for "spending their opulent means in aiding and giving comfort to ... Northern vandals." But Van Lew was unstoppable. She kept General Winder on her side because she could "flatter almost anything out of old Winder; his personal vanity is so great." She misled many other people by acting weird. "Crazy Bet" they called her, as she shuffled by humming out loud, singing, mumbling to herself. She wore tattered clothes and muddy shoes and let her unkempt curls bounce out from under her frayed bonnet.

But not everybody was fooled, and for four years

Elizabeth Van Lew had a secret room in her mansion. After Van Lew died, her niece recalled how she first discovered the room during the Civil War. The niece was living with Van Lew and one night she secretly followed her aunt to the top floor of the mansion. She watched Van Lew move a chest of drawers and press a hidden spring, which opened the door of a narrow, dark room. Suddenly a haggard-looking Union soldier crawled out of the darkness. Van Lew handed him a plate of food. Just then the niece noticed that the soldier had spotted her standing in the shadow behind her aunt. Quickly she put her finger to her lips and crept away. Later she returned and called to the soldier through the closed door. He told her how to press the secret spring. When the door opened, the soldier said, "My, what a spanking you would have got if your aunt had turned around!" After that Elizabeth Van Lew's niece decided that it was too dangerous to follow her mysterious aunt around—especially late at night! (Photo courtesy of the Valentine Museum, Richmond, Virginia.)

Van Lew and her mother lived in constant danger. "From the commencement of the war until its close, my life was in continued jeopardy . . . The threats, the scowls, the frowns of an infuriated community — who can write of them? I have had brave men shake their fingers in my face and say terrible things," she wrote in her journal, which she kept "buried for safety." (The journal was found in Van Lew's backyard after her death. Many sections had been cut out, apparently by Van Lew in order to protect people after the war. It is now in the New York Public Library.)

The risks were everywhere. Van Lew recorded some of them in her journal: "I have turned to speak to a friend and found a detective at my elbow. Strange faces could be seen peeping around the columns and pillars of the back portico . . . I shall ever remember the pale face of this dear lady [Van Lew's mother] . . . for her arrest was constantly spoken of, and frequently reported on the street, and some never hesitated to say she should be hanged . . . I always went to bed at night with anything dangerous on paper beside me, so as to be able to destroy it in a moment."

One threatening note was found with Van Lew's papers after she died. A crude skull and crossbones were drawn at the top of the paper. A childish drawing of a house on fire was at the bottom with "FIRE" written in big letters. The following warning with Van Lew's name misspelled was scrawled across the paper: "Mrs. Van Lough Look out for your fig bushes. There arn't much left of them now. White caps around town [the white caps were a secret proslavery society]. They are coming at night. Look out! Look out! Look out! Your house is going at last." It was signed, "White caps." A final sentence was scribbled at the bottom, "Please give me some of your blood to write with."

Elizabeth Van Lew had many close calls. Once she had to get critical information to Grant. She wrote a ciphered message, tore it into strips, and then rolled each strip into a tiny ball. The message was ready but Van Lew could not find a messenger. Time was running out. Grabbing her big basket, Van Lew headed for the market. Perhaps she would spot an agent there. Suddenly a passerby whispered, "I'm going through tonight!"

Was it a trap? Van Lew did not recognize the man. He could be a Union agent. Then, again, he could be a Confederate agent. Van Lew was not sure. He passed by again and whispered, "I'm going through the lines tonight!" Van Lew was desperate. She had to get the information to General Grant. But she just was not sure. She looked at the man's face. Should she trust him? "No!" she quickly decided. Darting down a side street, Elizabeth Van Lew hurried home.

She saw the man again. The next day, he went marching past her house with a regiment of Confederate soldiers.

After the Civil War began, this three-story warehouse in Richmond, Virginia, was converted into a prison for Union officers. Known as Libby Prison, it was an overcrowded, filthy, miserable place. For four years, Elizabeth Van Lew brought the Union prisoners food and supplies. During her visits, she gathered important military information. (Photo courtesy of the National Archives.)

On another occasion, soldiers came to her house looking for horses. Confederate soldiers were so desperate for horses that they would stop carriages in the streets and take horses right out of their harnesses. Now they had heard rumors that Van Lew had horses. She did—hidden in the basement. Calmly, Elizabeth Van Lew served the soldiers cake and tea. Then she had her servant take the soldiers to the basement. The servant took them the long way and fumbled to find the right key. Quickly and quietly, Van Lew led the horses up the wide basement stairs into the heavily carpeted dining room, where they finished off the cake.

Elizabeth Van Lew never lost her nerve. In one particularly bold move, she invited Captain George Gibbs, commander of Libby Prison, and his family to live in her house! As she explained in her journal, "so perilous had our situation become that we took him and his family to board with us. They were certainly a great protection . . ." She also managed to get one of her agents a job in President Jefferson Davis's White House! It was Mary Elizabeth Bowser, the former slave, who had returned from Philadelphia to help Van Lew. Although the records of her activities are lost, Bowser undoubtedly provided invaluable information.

All Van Lew's dispatches were written with a liquid that looked like water, which she kept in a small bottle. An application of milk made words written with the colorless liquid turn black. She set up five relay stations for getting information to Union officials. Her messengers carried ciphered messages in the soles of their shoes and inside hollowed out eggs that they placed among other eggs in a market basket. She had a wide network of agents, including her servants, a man called "Quaker," and women Van Lew identified only as Mrs. R. and Mrs. G. Her family was also involved. Without hesitation, they spent their fortune until it was gone.

From time to time, Van Lew hid people in a secret room in her mansion. Long, low, and narrow, the room was located on the upper floor under the sloping roof. The door, which was opened by pressing a secret spring, was hidden behind a chest of drawers.

Wearing a huge calico sunbonnet, buckskin leggings, and a one-piece cotton dress, Elizabeth Van Lew conducted various secret missions. One of her best-known exploits involved recovering the body of Colonel Ulric Dahlgren.

On February 28, 1864, Dahlgren was part of a raid on Richmond. Just a few months earlier, Dahlgren had lost part of his leg in battle. Now he was killed. Confederate soldiers cut off his finger to get a valuable ring and took his wooden leg and crutches (which were extremely valuable at that point in the war). They also supposedly found documents that proved Dahlgren planned to burn and sack Richmond and kill Jefferson Davis. People in Richmond were outraged. According to a newspaper, Dahlgren was given "a dog's burial, without coffin, winding sheet or service." The location of Dahlgren's grave was kept a secret.

But Elizabeth Van Lew found out where he was buried. Enlisting a group of men, she organized a rescue party, "which all knew was perilous in no small degree." They dug up Dahlgren's body, put it in a metal coffin, loaded it on a wagon, and covered it with young peach trees. Then "Mr. Rowley took the driver's seat and drove all that remained of the brave young Dahlgren through the several pickets ...", Van Lew recorded in her journal.

Dahlgren was reburied in a safe place with a peach tree planted over him. After the war, his family buried him again close to home.

Just months after Dahlgren died, Union troops advanced on Richmond again. Van Lew wrote, "As the war advanced and the army closed around Richmond, I was able to communicate with General Butler and General Grant, but not so well and persistently with General Butler, for there was too much danger in the system and person. With General Grant . . . I was more fortunate." Grant was also fortunate. For along with critical information, Van Lew sent him flowers from her garden, which appeared on his breakfast table every day.

On April 2, 1865, Confederate General Robert E. Lee told Jefferson Davis to evacuate Richmond. The Union troops would be there soon. Before they left, Confederate troops set fire to the tobacco warehouses. They did not want the Union to benefit from the sale of the valuable tobacco. Flames shot up. Suddenly a strong wind started blowing. In a flash, the fire spread. It burned all night. In the early morning hours, a powder magazine blew up, shattering windows all over town. Then an arsenal exploded, sending shells flying. People fled in terror.

Taking a great risk, Elizabeth Van Lew and her servants climbed to the top of her mansion. High above the burning city, they unfurled the Union flag—the first flag with stars and stripes to wave over Richmond in four years.

General Grant sent his aide, Colonel Parke, to protect Elizabeth Van Lew. Parke found her in the deserted Confederate Capitol building. She was searching for any documents that might help the Union. Although the war was over in Richmond, Elizabeth Van Lew was still finding ways to serve her country.

Chapter 4

THE SIREN OF THE SHENANDOAH

I would rather lie down in this prison and die ...

To the west of Richmond lay the Shenandoah Valley. It was a lush, fertile region. "The horses and cattle were fat and sleek; the large barns were flowing with the gathered crops ... It was truly a land of milk and honey," wrote one Confederate soldier. Prosperous villages and towns ran the length of the valley—Front Royal, Shepherdstown, New Market, and Port Republic. Throughout the valley, most people were devoted to Virginia and the South. And as soon as Virginia seceded, the men of the valley proudly put on the grey uniforms of the Confederacy.

The Union wanted to capture the Shenandoah Valley. They finally got it, but it was not easy. Back and forth, both sides struggled to control the valley and its rich resources. One town—Winchester—changed hands more than seventy times! The Union troops were not prepared to fight against such determined soldiers. They also were not prepared to deal with a seventeen-year-old girl—Belle Boyd. Fearless to the point of appearing reckless, vivacious to the point of appearing outrageous, Belle Boyd became the most famous spy of the war, for either side.

Everything about Belle Boyd's face was prominent —her high cheekbones, broad forehead, long face, wide lips, and large nose. Her eyes were grey-blue and her long, curly hair was golden brown. Tall and slender,

Boyd had, according to everyone who met her, a perfect figure. In the words of one man, she was "a splendid specimen of feminine health and vigor."

Her personality was as prominent as her features. After escorting her to a dance, a captain described her as, "possessing an originality and vivacity, no-care-madcap-devil-of-a temperament that pleases me." Belle Boyd was well-educated, witty, and warm. She was also an expert horseback rider—"a splendid and reckless rider of unflinching courage," according to Confederate Major Harry Gilmor.

Belle Boyd grew up in Martinsburg, Virginia (now in West Virginia), just twenty miles from the northern end of the Shenandoah Valley. When she was twelve, her parents sent her to Mount Washington Female College in Baltimore, Maryland. For four years, she studied classical literature, music, singing, and French. After Belle Boyd graduated, she went to Washington, D.C., where she participated in the lively social scene (undoubtedly, she met Rose O'Neal Greenhow).

Belle Boyd was totally devoted to the South. She was convinced that the North was out to conquer the South and to control the way Southerners lived and did business. When the Civil War started, Belle Boyd left Washington and returned to Martinsburg. Shortly after she arrived, her father, Ben, joined Company D, Second Virginia Infantry. It was one of the five regiments commanded by General Thomas Jonathan "Stonewall" Jackson. Unable to enlist because of her sex, Belle Boyd threw herself into raising money to buy arms and equipment for the soldiers.

On July 3, 1861, the sounds of battle were heard in Martinsburg. By 10:00 A.M., Jackson's troops, including her father, hustled through the town. They were retreating from Union troops under General Robert Patterson. Soon the Union troops occupied Martinsburg. The Union fife and drum corps played. Cavalry soldiers with elegant plumes waving from their hats rode by. The infantry marched with their muskets and bayonets. Wagons rolled by loaded with artillery and supplies. The next day was the Fourth of July, the first one with the United States split apart.

The Union troops celebrated the Fourth wildly in Martinsburg. Troops paraded. Bands played patriotic music. Soldiers drank toasts. Fights broke out. Windows were broken. Shots were fired. A group of Union soldiers heard that there were Confederate flags at the Boyds' house. And in fact, there were, all over the walls of Belle's room. Fortunately for Belle, Eliza, the Boyd's slave and Belle's personal servant, slipped upstairs before the soldiers and got rid of the flags.

Frustrated by not finding the flags, the soldiers had another idea. They decided to raise the Union flag over the Boyds' house. "Men, every member of my household will die before that flag shall be raised over us!" Mary Boyd, Belle's mother, warned them in a quiet, firm voice. A soldier threatened her. "I could stand it no longer," Belle Boyd wrote later. "My indignation was aroused beyond control, my blood was literally boiling in my veins. I drew my pistol and shot him."

The soldier died. Union officials conducted an impartial investigation. They decided that Belle Boyd had been "perfectly right" to defend herself and her mother. Belle Boyd was free — but not really. Union officers posted guards at her house. They wanted to keep an eye on Belle Boyd.

She quickly charmed her guards. Eager to please her, the Union soldiers talked too much. Before long, Belle Boyd and Eliza were taking secret messages to General Jackson and other Confederate military leaders. Boyd usually hid the message in the back of her watch case.

Unfortunately, Belle Boyd did not encipher her messages nor disguise her handwriting or her name. Within a week of shooting the soldier, she was standing before Union officials. They had intercepted one of her messages. A furious colonel berated her. He also read the Articles of War in case she did not know that death was the penalty for helping "the enemies of the United States Government ..." Bowing low, Belle Boyd replied in a mocking voice, "Thank you, gentlemen of the jury."

Belle Boyd's parents sent her to stay with her aunt and uncle, Frances and James Stewart, in Front Royal, Virginia, about seventy miles away. At the northern end of the Shenandoah Valley, Front Royal was a lovely village. Belle Boyd's aunt ran the Fishback Hotel. With their two daughters, they lived in a two-story cottage behind the hotel. Belle Boyd was there when the Confederates won the first battle of Bull Run (Manassas). She nursed wounded soldiers who were sent to the hospital in Front Royal.

In August 1861, Belle Boyd and her mother visited the Confederate camp at Bull Run (Manassas). It was there that Belle Boyd was appointed as a courier in the Confederate intelligence service. Riding her favorite horse, Fleeter, she carried information between Confederate Generals Jackson and Beauregard, and other officers. Belle Boyd had trained Fleeter to kneel — a useful trick when they had to duck from sight.

By the spring of 1862, Belle Boyd was back in Front Royal with her relatives. Union and Confederate troops continued to battle back and forth. Worried about her mother, Belle Boyd decided to take the train to Martinsburg. On the way, she was arrested. Again.

"I regret to say orders have been issued for your detention," Union Captain Bannon told her. With that, Belle Boyd was whisked off the train and taken to Baltimore. But she didn't stay there long. After a week in detention, she was released by General John A. Dix, the same general who dealt with Rose O'Neal Greenhow.

Although Dix freed her, the Union troops watched Belle Boyd closely when she returned to Martinsburg. In fact, they refused to let her leave the village. Finally, on May 12, 1862, Belle Boyd managed to wrangle travel passes for her and her mother to go to Richmond, Virginia.

Arriving at night, they discovered that the hotel had been taken over by Union General Shields and his staff. Belle Boyd and her mother had dinner with their relatives in the house behind the hotel. As daring as ever, Belle Boyd sent her calling card to General Shields. Without hesitation, he came to see her, bringing with him his aide-de-camp, Captain Daniel J. Keily. Fluent in four languages, Shields was a charming, witty man.

A few nights later, Belle Boyd went to the hotel to visit Shields and Keily. But they were busy meeting with other officers in the hotel drawing room. Slipping upstairs, she went into a bedroom located over the drawing room. Discovering a knothole in the floor, Belle Boyd put her ear to the hole and listened to them plan military maneuvers. Two hours later, she returned to her room and enciphered a message. Then she sneaked out to the stable, saddled a horse, and headed off to find Colonel Ashby, head of all the Confederate cavalry in the Shenandoah Valley. Riding hard for fifteen miles, Belle Boyd stopped at a friend's house, where she thought she might find Ashby. She rode her horse up the front steps and banged on the door.

Finally, she was let in. In an account she wrote later, Belle Boyd recorded what happened next.

"My dear, where did you come from, and how on earth did you get here?" her friend asked.

"Oh, I forced the sentries and here I am," Belle Boyd replied. "I must see Colonel Ashby ..."

The friend told her that Colonel Ashby was up the road a bit.

Mounting her horse, Belle Boyd prepared to ride off again. Just then Ashby appeared. "Good God! Miss Belle, is this you? Where did you come from? Have you dropped from the clouds, or am I dreaming?"

Belle Boyd quickly explained, gave Ashby the ciphered message, and galloped off into the night. Dashing by a series of sleepy Union sentries, Belle Boyd got home just before dawn. Exhausted, she collapsed in bed.

It was a time of intense military maneuvering. Union General McClellan was closing in on Richmond. For his final push, he wanted reinforcement from Union troops in the Shenandoah Valley. But Confederate General Stonewall Jackson was determined to keep the Union troops too busy to leave. In a series of surprising maneuvers, he defeated three separate Union armies in five battles.

One of those battles took place at Front Royal. Belle Boyd was there. So was G.W. Clarke, a Union reporter for the *New York Herald* newspaper, and a man who had annoyed Belle Boyd with inappropriate advances. The Union army was in control of the town.

On the evening of May 23, 1862, word spread that Confederate troops were approaching. Questioning a Union soldier, Belle Boyd discovered the Union's battle plan. Knowing that she had critical information, Belle Boyd got her opera-glasses and went to the balcony to check the Confederates' position. On the way, she passed Clarke's room. The key was in the door. "The temptation of making a Yankee prisoner was too strong to be resisted," Belle Boyd later wrote. Yielding to the impulse, she locked Clarke in his room!

The Confederate troops were less than a mile way, and her father was with them. Hurrying outside, Belle Boyd tried to get several men to take her message. They refused.

"I did not stop to reflect . . ." she recalled later. "I put on a white sun-bonnet, and started at a run down the street . . . I soon cleared the town and gained the open fields . . ." Wearing a dark-blue dress, with a little fancy white apron, Belle Boyd made an easy target. "My escape was most providential . . .", Belle Boyd wrote later, "the rifle-balls flew thick and fast about me, and more than one struck the ground so near my feet as to throw the dust in my eyes."

A teenager when the Civil War began, Belle Boyd gained international fame for her daring dash across a battlefield to give military information to Confederate General "Stonewall" Jackson. Newspaper reporters from France dubbed her "La Belle Rebelle." (Photo courtesy of Laura Virginia Hale Archives, Warren Heritage Society, Front Royal, Virginia.)

Belle Boyd's aunt and uncle, Frances and James Stewart, lived in Front Royal, Virginia, about seventy miles from Boyd's home in Martinsburg. They lived in this cottage located behind the Fishback Hotel, which they operated. Belle Boyd conducted several of her spying exploits from this house. Today the cottage is preserved as a historic landmark. (Photo courtesy of Laura Virginia Hale Archives, Warren Heritage Society, Front Royal, Virginia.)

Bullets whistled by her ears and pierced her clothing. Then an artillery shell hit close by, and Belle Boyd hit the ground. "Springing up when the danger was passed, I pursued my career, still under a heavy fire. I shall never run again as I ran on that, to me, memorable day." Motivated by "hope, fear, the love of life, and the determination to serve my country," Belle Boyd reached the Confederate troops.

She waved her bonnet and the troops cheered. Major Harry Douglas, an old friend, rode up. Douglas later described what happened next: "Nearly exhausted, and with her hand pressed against her heart, she said in gasps, 'I knew it must be Stonewall, when I heard the first gun. Go back quick and tell him that the Yankee force is very small ... Tell him, I know, for I went through the camps and got it out of an officer. Tell him to charge right down and he will catch them all. I must hurry back. Goodby. My love to all the dear boys — and remember if you meet me in town you haven't seen me today."

Jackson did charge right down and chase the Yankees out of town. Although Clarke escaped through his window after Boyd locked him in, he was still captured. "I'll make you rue this," he shouted at Belle Boyd as he was led away.

After the fighting, Douglas went looking for Belle Boyd. He found her "talking with some few Federal officers [prisoners] ... Her cheeks were rosy with excitement and recent exercise, and her eyes all aflame ... as I stooped from my saddle she pinned a crimson rose to my uniform, bidding me remember that it was *blood-red* and that it was her 'colors.'"

After leaving some soldiers to hold the town, General Jackson moved on. Within a week, Union troops recaptured Front Royal and captured Belle Boyd. But not for long. As soon as Union General Shields arrived, he released her.

Throughout the North and South, Belle Boyd's exploit at Front Royal made the newspapers. Finally the

Federal government in Washington decided to do something about Belle Boyd. A Union scout, C.W.D. Smitley, was assigned to trap her. Arriving in Front Royal disguised as a paroled Confederate officer, Smitley later reported "that Miss Boyd was the sensation of the village, that the intensely loyal Confederates idolized her, and that she had a large following of Federal officers who were ready to do her homage." Smitley met Boyd and found her to be "a lady of culture, a brilliant conversationalist, expert with the piano, and rather pretty."

Fooled by Smitley, Belle Boyd asked him to deliver a letter full of military information to Stonewall Jackson. Once again, Belle Boyd was arrested. This time, guarded by 450 cavalrymen, she was taken by carriage to Winchester; then to Martinsburg, where she saw her mother; then by train to Washington. A crowd of reporters and onlookers met her train. Quickly detectives whisked her away to Old Capitol Prison, the same place Rose O'Neal Greenhow had been imprisoned. "And so this is the celebrated rebel spy. I am very glad to see you, and will endeavor to make you as comfortable as possible," William Wood, the prison superintendent, greeted her.

On the evening of her first day, Wood and Lafayette Baker, chief of detectives, tried to get her to swear an oath of allegiance to the United States Government. Boyd refused. "I would rather lie down in this prison and die, than leave it owning allegiance to such a government as yours. Now leave the room; for so thoroughly am I disgusted with your conduct towards me, that I cannot endure your presence longer." As she finished, Boyd heard cheers and applause from the other prisoners. After Wood and Baker left, a minute nutshell basket painted with miniature Confederate flags was tossed into Boyd's cell by a fellow prisoner.

Belle Boyd made quite an impression while she was in prison. She put up a picture of Confederate President Davis. A guard tore it down and confined her to her room during the worst of the stifling summer heat. She exchanged information with other prisoners and visitors. She waved a Confederate flag out of her window.

And she sang a favorite Confederate song, "Maryland! My Maryland!" Later a former prisoner recalled, "She would sing that song as if her very soul was in every word she uttered. It used to bring a lump up in my throat every time I heard it. It seemed like my heart was ready to jump out — as if I could put my finger down and touch it ..."

After a month, Union officials released Belle Boyd and exiled her to Richmond. From Richmond, her father took her back to Martinsburg. Soon she left to visit friends and relatives in Tennessee, Alabama, and Georgia. She was a hero everywhere she went. One Southern newspaper called her the "fair and fearless Virginia" and praised her "invaluable services in conveying information ..."

Belle Boyd returned to Martinsburg in June of 1863. Confederate troops finally pushed Union troops out of the valley. Then they marched off with General Robert E. Lee to invade Pennsylvania. Although "Stonewall" Jackson and other brilliant Confederate military leaders had died, Southerners still thought they would win the war. Then Confederate troops suffered a terrible defeat at the Battle of Gettysburg. The line of wounded soldiers seeking care stretched to Martinsburg and beyond. Belle Boyd nursed soldiers in her home. She also took care of her father, who was recuperating from battle fatigue, and her mother, who had just had a baby. Suddenly, the Union troops arrived again. Within days, Belle Boyd was arrested. Again.

Ben Boyd requested that his daughter be allowed to stay until her mother recovered. Agreeing, Union officials confined her to her home. One day Captain James Stevenson came to talk to Belle Boyd. He later reported that she showed him her Confederate uniform —a gray skirt; gray cloth jacket, slashed with gold lace at the breast and sleeves; white buckskin gauntlets; a dove-colored soft felt hat with a long plume; and a leather belt with a silver-handled pistol in a leather case.

Finally, Belle Boyd was sent back to Washington. This time she was put in Carroll Prison, which was connected with Old Capitol. One night she was amazed to see an arrow zip through her window with a note fastened to it and signed, C.H. The note informed her that she had friends in Washington. It also said the archer would come on Thursday and Saturday and whistle a particular tune. If Belle Boyd thought it was safe, she should turn down her gas light and stand away from the window. Then the archer would shoot another arrow with a message. Belle Boyd was instructed to get a large rubber ball, cut it open, put an answer inside, sew it back together, and then throw it out the window. Thus, Belle Boyd and the archer began exchanging messages. Once the arrow brought her Confederate flags, which she put up in her cell.

This prison stay was harder and longer. Belle Boyd suffered a serious attack of typhoid fever. After recovering, she learned she had been sentenced to do hard labor at Fitchburg jail. Fortunately, Belle Boyd's father had enough connections in Washington to get her sentence changed to "banishment to the South — never to return North again during the war." Belle Boyd left prison on December 2, 1863. Shortly after she arrived in Richmond, she received news that her father had died. Belle Boyd was devastated.

In bad health and grieving, Belle Boyd went on a second tour of the South. In March of 1864, she returned to Richmond and agreed to carry Confederate dispatches to Europe. She left Wilmington, North Carolina on the steamer *Greyhound*. Loaded down with cotton, money, secret papers, tobacco, and turpentine, the *Greyhound* tried to run the blockade. It did not make it. Belle Boyd was captured again. In the official records she was listed as the "famous rebel lady."

A Union officer, Samuel Hardinge, took command of

the *Greyhound* and sailed it to Boston. On the way, Samuel Hardinge fell in love with Belle Boyd. Belle Boyd later explained what happened to a newspaper reporter: "He fell in love with me on the trip North and asked me to marry him. I said I would if he would agree to give me his signal book, covering every flag of the United States naval code, leave the navy, enter the service of the confederacy, and help the captain of the *Greyhound* to escape . . . He accepted the conditions and I received the signal book."

Hardinge did everything he promised. The United States Navy dismissed him for "neglect of duty." His father disinherited him. Belle Boyd was banished to Canada. From there she sailed to London, England. Hardinge joined her there, and they were married. Shortly after the wedding, Boyd wrote to President Jefferson Davis: ". . . I trust from my having married a man of Northern birth my Country will not doubt my loyalty . . . If at any time I can be of benefit to my Country, command me."

Boyd stayed in England while Hardinge returned to fight for the Confederacy, but he was arrested by Union officials. In an effort to free Hardinge, Belle Boyd wrote a letter to President Abraham Lincoln: "I have heard from good authority that if I suppress the Book I have now ready for publication, you may be induced to consider leniently the case of my husband . . . I think it would be well for you & me to come to some definite understanding . . ." It is not known whether or not Lincoln was worried about the "atrocious circumstances" Boyd threatened to disclose in her book. But ten days after she sent her letter, Hardinge was released. Two months later, the war was over. The South had surrendered. Belle Boyd was twenty-one years old. Her career as the Siren of the Shenandoah, as one newspaper called her, was over. But not before she had been arrested and confined six to seven times, reported over thirty times, and imprisoned twice.

Years after the Civil War ended, Belle Boyd supported herself and her children by performing a show about her Civil War adventures. She wore a costume modeled after a Confederate officer's uniform and billed herself, "The Rebel Spy." Her show was a big hit, and she ended every performance by acknowledging the Union's victory with the words: "One God. One Flag. One People—Forever." (Photo courtesy of Laura Virginia Hale Archives, Warren Heritage Society, Front Royal, Virginia.)

Chapter 5

GENERAL TUBMAN

I never saw such a sight.

When the Civil War started, most black people were slaves, but some were free. They had run away to freedom in the North or found ways to earn money and buy their own freedom. Other slaves had been freed by their owners (like Mary Elizabeth Bowser had been freed by Elizabeth Van Lew; see Chapter 3). All together there were 488,000 free black people in the United States. Many of them wanted to fight for the Union. One group of free black men wrote in a resolution to the government: "... we are ready to stand by and defend our Government as the equals of its white defenders; to do so with our lives, our fortunes, and our sacred honor ..."

But the Union did not want them to be soldiers. President Abraham Lincoln worried that the sight of black soldiers would upset the border states, as slave states (Maryland, Delaware, Kentucky, and Missouri) that had remained in the Union were called. It might even cause them to leave the Union.

There were also many military leaders, including President Lincoln, who did not think black people would be good fighters. They were wrong. One of the best fighters black or white was Harriet Tubman, a former slave who served heroically as a nurse, scout, and spy.

Even before the war began, Harriet Tubman was a hero. Since her escape from slavery in 1849, Tubman had slipped back into slave territory about nineteen times and brought more than 300 slaves to freedom. She was so effective that the state of Maryland offered $12,000 for her capture. A group of slave owners once offered $40,000! She was called "Moses," after the prophet in the Bible who led his people out of slavery in Egypt. She was also called General Tubman.

Toughened by years of hard labor, Harriet Tubman was a powerful woman. According to one account, "before she was nineteen years old she was a match for the strongest man on the plantation ... She could lift huge barrels of produce and draw a loaded stone boat like an ox." About five feet tall, Harriet Tubman had formidable features—heavy-lidded, wide-set, dark eyes, strong cheekbones and forehead, and a firm mouth with a full lower lip (she had lost her upper front teeth, so her upper lip appeared flat). Her only receding feature was her chin, and that was balanced by her well-defined ears.

Harriet Tubman wore a colorful bandanna, which covered her short hair, tightly wrapped around her head. It also covered a sizeable dent in her head. Tubman was not born with a dent in her head. It was put there by a slave overseer when Tubman was trying to protect a runaway slave. She was a teenager when the incident happened.

It happened at the end of a long, hard day of work in a farmer's field. Suddenly Tubman noticed one of the other slaves slip away. The overseer saw him leave, too. Chasing the slave to a store, the overseer cornered him and ordered Tubman and the other slaves to tie him up for a whipping. Harriet Tubman refused, and the runaway jumped up and ran out the door. The enraged overseer picked up a two-pound weight from the counter and threw it at the runaway slave. He missed and hit Harriet Tubman instead. Her head cracked open, blood gushed out, and Harriet Tubman collapsed in a heap.

It took Harriet Tubman a long time to recover, but she did. For the rest of her life, though, she suffered from severe headaches and seizures that caused her suddenly to fall asleep. In the middle of a conversation, while working, or even while walking, Harriet Tubman would fall sound asleep. After a short time, she would wake up and go on as if nothing had happened.

Harriet Tubman escaped from slavery when she was about twenty-nine years old. Years later, she recalled her reaction when she crossed the border into Pennsylvania, a free state: "... I looked at my hands to see if I was the same person. There was such a glory over everything; the sun came like gold through the trees, and over the fields, and I felt like I was in Heaven."

Determined to rescue her family and friends, Tubman became a conductor on the Underground Railroad, a secret network of people who helped escaping slaves reach freedom in the Northern states or Canada. For about ten years, Harriet Tubman led slaves to freedom. During this time, she perfected all the skills she would use during the Civil War. She devised and implemented plans. She avoided detection, including outsmarting the bloodhounds slave owners used to track runaway slaves. She commanded groups of people. According to one person, Harriet Tubman "could not read or write but she had military genius."

Harriet Tubman was tough. When one escaping slave lost his nerve and wanted to quit, Tubman aimed her pistol at his head and said, "Move or die!" She was resourceful. Once she heard a group of men talking about capturing her. Quickly Tubman pretended to read a book that she carried, hoping that she had it right side up! After remarking that the Harriet Tubman they were looking for could not read or write, the men ignored her. And she was bold. It was not unusual for her to hitch up an unsuspecting slave owner's horse and buggy, hide escaping slaves in it, and drive away.

As soon as the war began, Harriet Tubman was

involved. First she probably went to Maryland and Virginia to help contraband, or fugitive, slaves who came to the Union army for protection. As the war continued, more slaves escaped. Slave owners thought that the Union army should return the runaway slaves. But Union General Benjamin Butler declared that they were "contraband of war"—property that was illegal for slave owners to have—and refused to return them.

South Carolina—the first state to secede from the Union—had the largest number of contraband, in particular on the Sea Islands at the southern end of South Carolina. Located between Charleston, South Carolina and Savannah, Georgia, the Sea Islands were formed where several rivers came together and cut through the land to the Atlantic Ocean. The island had large plantations where slaves grew rice, cotton, and tobacco. Beaufort was a beautiful and important port on Port Royal Island.

In November 1861, Union troops captured Port Royal Island and gained control of the Sea Islands. The plantation owners fled, and thousands of slaves escaped to the Union army. Major General David Hunter had his headquarters on Port Royal Island and needed someone to serve as a liaison with the contraband. He also needed an expert scout and spy for his military operations. When Massachusetts Governor John Andrew heard about Hunter's situation, he suggested Harriet Tubman. With Andrew's endorsement, Tubman traveled to Beaufort onboard the Union ship *Atlantic*.

Hunter welcomed her warmly and assigned her to the headquarters of General Stevens. One of the passes Hunter gave Tubman so that she could safely cross Union lines read: "Pass the bearer, Harriet Tubman ... and give her free passage at all times, on all Government transports. Harriet was sent to me from Boston by Governor Andrew, of Massachusetts, and is a valuable woman. She has permission, as a servant of the Government, to purchase such provisions from the

Commissary as she may need."

At first, Tubman devoted her energies to nursing contraband and white Union soldiers. Famous for the remedies she prepared, Harriet Tubman traveled to hospitals in South Carolina, Georgia, and Florida. Her medicines saved the lives of many sick people. She also cared for wounded soldiers.

"I'd go to the hospital early every morning," she recalled later. "I'd get a big chunk of ice and put it in a basin, and fill it with water; then I'd take a sponge and begin. First man I'd come to, I'd thrash away the flies, and they'd rise, like bees around a hive. Then I'd begin to bathe their wounds, and by the time I'd bathed off three or four, the fire and heat would have melted the ice and made the water warm, and it would be as red as clear blood. Then I'd go and get more ice, and by the time I got to the next one, the flies would be around the first ones black and thick as ever."

Shortly after Harriet Tubman arrived, General Hunter issued a proclamation freeing all the slaves in Georgia, South Carolina, and Florida. Still worried about the border states, President Lincoln quickly overruled Hunter's proclamation. Next General Hunter decided to recruit a regiment of contraband, the 1st South Carolina Volunteers. That caused a furor in Congress. Within three months, the regiment was disbanded and Hunter was replaced by General Rufus Saxton.

Finally the North started to change its mind about black soldiers. The war had gone on much longer than people expected. The North was losing battles. Growing numbers of white soldiers were deserting. Abolitionists were increasing their pressure on President Lincoln to end slavery. "This is no time to fight with only your white hand, and allow your black hand to remain tied," wrote Frederick Douglass, a famous black abolitionist.

In July 1862, Congress passed an act that allowed free black men to enlist as soldiers. In August, General Saxton started to form five regiments of contraband to be commanded by white officers. He invited his friend Colonel Thomas Wentworth Higginson to command a regiment, the 1st South Carolina Volunteers (the same name as Hunter's disbanded regiment). "It was an offer that took my breath away, and fulfilled the dream of a lifetime," Higginson, an ardent abolitionist, confided in his diary.

Tubman was glad to see Higginson. They had worked together in Boston, Massachusetts, and were old friends. She also welcomed Colonel James Montgomery, who came to lead another black regiment, the 2nd South Carolina Volunteers. A fierce antislavery fighter, Montgomery was an expert in guerrilla warfare.

About the time Higginson and Montgomery arrived, Harriet Tubman organized a unit of scouts and spies to operate from South Carolina to Florida. With herself as commander, Tubman handpicked nine black scouts and river pilots: Isaac Hayward, Walter Plowden, Gabriel Cahern, George Chisholm, Peter Burns, Mott Blake, Sandy Sellus, Charles Simmons, and Samuel Hayward. They made repeated trips up the rivers and into the swamps, marshes, and jungles to obtain information about Confederate troop strength and defenses. They also surveyed plantations and Southern towns, looking for slaves whom they could enlist in the Union army.

Tubman's information was invaluable. At one point, General Saxton wrote to Secretary of War Edwin Stanton about conducting a Union attack on Jacksonville, Florida, because, "I have reliable information that there are large numbers of able bodied Negroes in that vicinity who are watching for an opportunity to join us." Undoubtedly Saxton was referring to Tubman's "reliable information." A few days later, Union troops did capture Jacksonville.

As soon as Montgomery trained his black troops, he started conducting river raids. The success of the missions depended on Tubman's information. By all accounts the raids were very successful. According to

Higginson, "In Colonel Montgomery's hands these up-river raids reached the dignity of a fine art ... I remember being on the wharf ... when he came down from his first trip. The steamer seemed an animated hen-coop. Live poultry hung from the foremast shrouds, dead ones from the mainmast, geese hissed from the binnacle, a pig paced the quarter-deck and a duck's wings were seen fluttering from a line ..."

On June 2, 1863, Harriet Tubman and James Montgomery conducted one of the most successful raids up the Combahee River. The raid lasted all night and through the morning of the next day. Tubman and Montgomery took three gunboats. The object was to remove enemy torpedoes from the river, destroy railroads and bridges, capture supplies, and free slaves on the plantations. A narrow, wiggly river, the Combahee was lined with marshes and rice fields.

Confederate pickets spotted the gunboats at the mouth of the river. But Tubman and Montgomery kept going. At every plantation or Confederate picket post, a small group of soldiers would leave the gunboat in a small boat and row ashore. They had no trouble routing the Confederate pickets or setting fire to the plantation. At first the slaves were afraid. Then they flocked to the river.

Later Tubman recalled the scene, "I never saw such a sight. We laughed and laughed and laughed. Here you'd see a woman with a pail on her head, rice a-smoking in it just as she'd taken it from the fire, young one hanging on behind, one hand around her forehead to hold on, the other hand digging into the rice pot, eating with all its might; a-hold of her dress two or three more; down her back a bag with a pig in it. One woman brought two pigs, a white and a black one; we took them all on board; named the white pig Beauregard [Confederate general], and the black pig Jeff Davis [Confederate president].

Loaded down with supplies and freed slaves, the

gunboats returned to Beaufort. Montgomery made a speech. Everybody sang a song. Then Tubman spoke.

A newspaper reporter wrote about the Combahee raid in an article for *The Commonwealth*, a Boston, Massachusetts newspaper:

HARRIET TUBMAN

Col. Montgomery and his gallant band of 300 black soldiers, under the guidance of a black woman, dashed into the enemy's country, struck a bold and effective blow, destroying millions of dollars worth of commissary stores, cotton and lordly dwellings, and striking terror into the heart of rebeldom, brought off near 800 slaves and thousands of dollars worth of property, without losing a man or receiving a scratch. It was a glorious consummation.

After they were all fairly well disposed of in the Beaufort charge, they were addressed in strains of thrilling eloquence by their gallant deliverer, to which they responded in a song "There is a white robe for thee," a song so appropriate and so heartfelt and cordial as to bring unbidden tears.

The Colonel was followed by a speech from the black woman, who led the raid and under whose inspiration it was originated and conducted. For sound sense and real native eloquence, her address would do honor to any man, and it created a great sensation ...

Many and many times she has penetrated the enemy's lines and discovered their situation and condition, and escaped without injury, but not without extreme hazard.

One unexpected consequence of the Combahee expedition was that Tubman decided to wear bloomers, or baggy pants. In a letter a fellow soldier wrote for her (Tubman could not read or write), Tubman explained and asked a friend in Boston to have "the ladies" (a sewing group) send her a pair of bloomers:

68

Harriet Tubman frequent-ly wore a bandanna tightly wrapped around her head. The strength and power of her character is clearly captured in this photograph. (Photo courtesy of A.M.E. Church, Harriet Tubman Home, Auburn, New York.)

After her Civil War service, Harriet Tubman returned to her home in Auburn, New York. Tubman had very few possessions, but her friends provided her with a beautiful bed and clock. Propped up beside Tubman's bed is a large Bible with a leather cover. Unable to read herself, Tubman loved to listen as her friends read the Bible out loud. (Courtesy of A.M.E. Zion Home, Auburn, New York. Photographs by Penny Colman.)

In our late expedition up the Combahee River, in coming on board the boat, I was carrying two pigs for a poor sick woman, who had a child to carry, and the order 'double quick' was given, and I started to run, stepped on my dress, it being rather long, and fell and tore it almost off, so that when I got on board the boat, there was hardly anything left of it but shreds. I made up my mind then I would never wear a long dress on another expedition of the kind, but would have a bloomer as soon as I could get it. So please make this known to the ladies, if you will, for I expect to have use for it very soon, probably before they can get it to me.

Harriet Tubman did go on other raids. According to General Saxton, "She made many raids inside the enemy's lines, displaying remarkable courage, zeal, and fidelity." Finally in May of 1864, she returned North to check on her elderly parents. While she was there, she became ill. She was totally exhausted and her sleeping seizures became worse.

The war was over before Harriet Tubman was strong enough to return to the front lines. But Harriet Tubman was content. She knew she had served her country well. So did the white military men who had served with her. In the words of Colonel James Montgomery, Harriet Tubman was "a most remarkable woman, and invaluable scout."

Chapter 6

MANY MORE SPIES

I was ready to start on my first secret expedition ...

Union and Confederate women spies were a diverse bunch of people. Belle Boyd was a teenager. Harriet Tubman, Rose O'Neal Greenhow, and Elizabeth Van Lew were in their forties. Tubman was an unschooled former slave. Greenhow, Van Lew, and Boyd were well-educated and wealthy. Boyd and Greenhow were flamboyant. Tubman and Van Lew were reserved. Boyd and Greenhow supported slavery. Tubman and Van Lew despised it.

The women spies had different styles and experiences. Van Lew and Greenhow headed extensive spy rings. Tubman led a small group of scouts. Boyd acted on her own. Greenhow and Boyd were imprisoned. Van Lew and Tubman weren't. Greenhow and Van Lew did not fire a shot. Tubman carried a rifle on her raids and most likely did fire shots. Belle Boyd killed a Union soldier. Van Lew spied continuously from the beginning until the end of the war. Tubman probably spied about two years. Boyd spied on and off, as did Greenhow until she died in the third year of the war.

Elizabeth Van Lew, Harriet Tubman, Belle Boyd, and Rose O'Neal Greenhow were not the only women Civil War spies. There were many more—Nancy Hart, Loreta Velazquez, Sarah Emma Edmonds, Pauline Cushman ...

Like Harriet Tubman, Nancy Hart never learned to

Nancy Hart was a prisoner when this picture was taken. A Union soldier who was smitten by Hart asked a photographer to take her picture. At first Hart refused because she did not have proper clothes. Determined to get the picture, the soldier borrowed a dress for Hart from another woman. Then he took a Union soldier's hat, rearranged the shape, decorated it with a feather and ribbon, and put it on her head. Perhaps that's why she looks so grim! (Photo courtesy of the West Virginia State Archives.)

read and write. Like Belle Boyd, she was a teenager and an expert rider. She also killed a Union soldier.

Just fifteen years old when the war started, Nancy Hart lived in the western part of Virginia. A land of narrow valleys and rugged mountains, western Virginia was separated from the rest of Virginia by the Allegheny Mountains. There were no plantations and very few slaves. When Virginia seceded from the Union, many people in western Virginia objected—so much so that they formed a new state, known today as West Virginia. Although West Virginia joined the Union, there were many Southern sympathizers in the area, and Confederate troops did not give up easily.

Nancy Hart and her family supported the South. When Hart's brother-in-law was killed, she left home and joined the Moccasin Rangers, a group of pro-Southern guerrillas. She could ride and shoot with the best of the men. Sturdy and fearless, Nancy Hart rode on guerrilla raids.

After one raid, Nancy Hart was captured and taken to the Union camp. She charmed the soldiers and fooled them into thinking she was harmless. They released her.

That was a mistake because Nancy Hart had spent her time in the Union camp learning everything she could about their troop strength and plans to defeat the guerrillas.

The Moccasin Rangers conducted a series of raids until the summer of 1862 when their leader was killed. The group disbanded, and Hart married Joshua Douglas, a former Ranger. Enlisting in the Confederate army, Douglas went off to fight. Nancy Hart went into the mountains to spy on the Union troops.

Posing as a simple country girl, Nancy Hart spent about a year gathering military information. Then one day a Union soldier recognized her. Arrested again, Nancy Hart was taken to Summersville, a town occupied by Union troops.

Once again Nancy Hart charmed the Union soldiers. In particular she charmed her guard. One day she talked him into letting her hold his gun. Smiling and talking, she raised the gun and pretended to take aim. Then she shot, killing the guard with a bullet through his heart. Racing outside, Nancy Hart jumped on the Union commander's fastest horse and galloped away. Union troops pursued her, but she outrode them.

A week later, just before sunrise, Nancy Hart returned to Summersville. This time she came with about 200 Confederate cavalrymen and chased the Union troops out of town. In the process, Hart and the Confederates captured several Union officers and sent them to Libby Prison in Richmond (where most likely they were comforted by Elizabeth Van Lew; see Chapter 3).

Loreta Janeta Velazquez also spied for the Confederacy. Born in Havana, Cuba, Velazquez grew up in New Orleans, Louisiana. She married a United States Army officer, who when the war started decided to fight for the Confederacy. According to a book she wrote after the war, Velazquez fought for the South, too. Although she may have exaggerated her adventures, her story is fascinating.

As Velazquez told the story, she disguised herself as a man by flattening her breasts with wire shields and braces and wearing an army uniform. Calling herself Harry T. Buford, Velazquez adopted a manly swagger, perfected the ability to spit, and organized a company of soldiers, the "Arkansas Grays." As a lieutenant of the company, Velazquez fought in several battles—the first battle at Bull Run (see Chapter 2 for Rose Greenhow's role), Ball's Bluff, and Shiloh. "Fear was a word I did not know the meaning of," Velazquez wrote later.

Living as a man among men, Velazquez concluded that their conversations were generally "revolting and utterly vile." She also reported that soldiers' talk about women was "thoroughly despicable."

By 1863, Velazquez's husband had been killed, she had been wounded twice, and her true sex had been discovered. At this point, Velazquez switched to spying. She claimed that she managed to work undetected on the staff of Union Colonel Lafayette C. Baker, chief of the United States Secret Services. She was also sent to Canada to spy. According to one account, Velazquez was "the beautiful Confederate spy whose black eyes bewitched passes from Union generals."

Sarah Emma Edmonds was another woman who started her Civil War service disguised as a man. Born in Canada, Edmonds had run away to the United States to avoid marrying a man her father had selected for her. Since she had a flat chest and deep voice, Edmonds decided to pass herself off as Franklin Thompson, a Bible salesman. When the war started, she enlisted as a male nurse. The day a soldier she loved was killed, Edmonds decided to avenge his death. She volunteered to undertake a dangerous spying mission.

In an account she wrote later, Edmonds reported that after she volunteered she was "questioned and cross-questioned with regard to my views of the rebellion and my motive in wishing to engage in so perilous an undertaking ... Next I was examined with regard to my knowledge of the use of firearms, and in that department I sustained my character in a manner worthy of a veteran."

Her mission was to obtain detailed information about fortifications the Confederates were building at Yorktown, Virginia. Edmonds knew that contraband were being hired to work on the fortifications, so she decided to disguise herself as a contraband. "I purchased a suit of contraband clothing, real plantation style, and then I went to a barber and had my hair sheared close to my head," she wrote later. "Next came the coloring process — head, face, neck, hands, and arms were colored black as any African ..."

Edmonds completed her disguise with a wig. Then, as she recalled later, "I was ready to start on my first secret expedition toward the Confederate capital . . . With a few hard crackers in my pocket, and my revolver loaded and capped, I started on foot . . . At half-past nine o'clock I passed through the outer picket line of the Union army, at twelve o'clock I was within the rebel lines ..."

The Confederates gave Edmonds a "pickaxe, shovel, and a monstrous wheelbarrow" and put her to work building an eight-foot parapet. At night she wrote reports and made sketches of the Confederate guns and defenses and hid them "under the inner sole of my contraband shoes ..." On the second day she was astonished to recognize a peddler who regularly visited the Union headquarters. Eavesdropping while he talked to Confederate officers, Edmonds heard him giving a "full description of our camp and forces." He also gave them a map and described how he had killed a Union officer. "I thanked God for that information," Edmonds wrote later. "He was a fated man from that moment; his life was not worth three cents ..."

On the night of the third day, Edmonds slipped away carrying a "splendid rifle." Then, Edmonds related later, "with the first dawn of morning I hoisted the well-known signal and was welcomed once more to a sight of the dear old stars and stripes ... I made out my report immediately and carried it to General McClellan's headquarters ..., together with my trophy (the rifle) from the land of traitors ..."

In 1863, Edmonds became ill with malaria. Fearing that doctors would discover her true gender, Edmonds deserted to avoid going to the hospital. After she recovered, she dropped her disguise as a man and worked in hospitals as a woman.

Although Sarah Emma Edmonds avoided being captured, another Union woman spy, Pauline Cushman, was not so lucky. In fact, Cushman was sentenced to be hanged!

Her spying career began in Louisville, Kentucky. One of the border states, Kentucky remained in the Union. However, it was a slave state and had a number of Southern supporters. Cushman was an actor who appeared at Wood's Theatre in Louisville. A Creole, Pauline Cushman was born Harriet Wood in New Orleans, Louisiana. Olive-skinned with full lips and blue-black hair, Cushman had a full figure that a newspaper reporter wrote was "perfect—so perfect that the sculptor's imagination would fail to add a single point, or banish a single blemish."

One night Pauline Cushman stopped her performance, stepped to the front of the stage, lifted a champagne glass she was holding, and shouted, "Here's to Jefferson Davis and the Southern Confederacy. May the South always maintain her honor and her rights."

Pandemonium broke out. Confederate sympathizers cheered. Union supporters booed. Then they started slugging each other. Pauline Cushman became the darling of the Confederacy. Too bad for them that they did not know she was a Union spy.

Cushman became a spy when two paroled Confederate officers tried to bribe her to toast Davis and the Confederacy. Cushman reported the bribe to Union officials, who advised her to accept it. Sitting in the au-

76

dience the night Cushman made her toast, the Union officials noted the people who revealed their Southern sympathies by cheering. Then they arrested Cushman and held her just long enough to fool the Confederates.

Before long, Southern supporters and spies began to contact her. Cushman became a expert in counterespionage, or spying on enemy spies. She made lists of Southern spies. She uncovered many of their tricks—how they sent messages inside dead chickens and the handles of knives. She also obtained information on when Confederate supplies were being shipped and how their guerrilla troops operated.

In the spring of 1863, Union officials asked her to get information about the Confederate troops under the command of General Braxton Bragg, a man known to treat spies harshly. Pretending that she was looking for her lost brother, Cushman followed Bragg's troops through Kentucky and Tennessee.

Then Cushman got careless. Confederate soldiers discovered incriminating papers that she had hidden in her shoe. She was arrested and taken to Shelbyville, Tennessee. General Bragg ordered her tried. Without hesitation, the court found her guilty and sentenced her to be hanged. To Cushman's great relief (also to the relief of a Confederate captain who had grown very fond of her), Union General Rosecrans and his troops attacked Shelbyville. The Confederate troops fled without Pauline Cushman.

The Union troops treated her like a hero. However, Cushman's brush with death left her badly shaken. In time she recovered and was awarded an honorary major's commission by President Abraham Lincoln. Her cover blown, Pauline Cushman returned to the stage. For the rest of the war, she presented monologues about her exploits.

Pauline Cushman, Sarah Emma Edmonds, Loreta Velazquez, Nancy Hart, Harriet Tubman, Belle Boyd, Elizabeth Van Lew, Rose O'Neal Greenhow—the list of

Pauline Cushman was the only woman spy who was caught and sentenced to be hanged. Happily, the day before she was due to die, Union troops routed her Confederate captors, who left her behind when they fled. President Abraham Lincoln named her an honorary major. After the war, Pauline Cushman presented dramatic monologues about her exploits. She is pictured here wearing her custom-made uniform. (Photo courtesy of the National Archives.)

women Civil War spies could go on and on. But, for this book, the list ends here. Hopefully readers will continue the list — Hattie Lawton, Mrs. E.M. Baker, Lucy Williams, Antonia Ford, Emmeline Piggot, Laura Ratcliffe ...

It will take some digging. All too many historians forgot to write about women's contributions, especially in such an unwomanly matter as spying! But the stories are there in military records, letters and diaries, old newspaper and magazine articles, and old books—the stories of committed, courageous, and clever women.

Chapter 7

AFTER THE WAR

She risked everything that is dear ...

No one expected the Civil War to last so long, spread so far, destroy so much property, or kill so many people. It lasted four full years; involved more than 2,200 battles; spread from South Carolina to Virginia, Minnesota, Florida, New Mexico, and Oregon; cost more than $8 billion; and resulted in more than one million casualties.

Rose O'Neal Greenhow was one of those casualties. As for the other women spies in this book, they all survived the war.

After the war, Nancy Hart lived a quiet life with her husband on a mountain farm. When she died in 1902, Nancy Hart was buried on a mountain crag. Her grave was marked with a pile of stones. Years later, her granddaughter went looking for Hart's grave. But Nancy Hart's grave was gone. Instead a beacon tower stood on the spot, which had been leveled by a bulldozer.

Belle Boyd died two years before Hart in 1900. Her postwar life was not so quiet. Two months after the war ended, Boyd published her book, *Belle Boyd in Camp and Prison*, had a daughter, and buried her husband. Needing to support herself and her daughter Grace, Boyd became an actor. Four years later, she married a wealthy businessman and had four more children (one died as an infant). After a period of happy years, Boyd's marriage ended in a divorce. She returned to the stage to support herself and her family.

Rose O'Neal Greenhow was buried with military honors in Oakdale Cemetery, Wilmington, North Carolina. Even today members of the United Daughters of the Confederacy tend Greenhow's grave and place flowers on it on May 10th of every year, which is Confederate Memorial Day in some southern states. Inscribed on the front of the headstone are the words: "Mrs. Rose O'N. Greenhow, a bearer of dispatches to the Confederate Government." Inscribed on the back are the words: "Drowned off Fort Fisher, from the Steamer Condor, while attempting to run the blockade. Sept. 30, 1864." (Photo courtesy of Oakdale Cemetery Company, Wilmington, North Carolina.)

Billing herself The Rebel Spy, Belle Boyd presented a "thrilling dramatic narrative" called *North and South Or The Perils of a Spy*. It was a hit with audiences throughout the United States. At the age of fifty-six, Belle Boyd died of a heart attack in Kilbourn (now known as Wisconsin Dells), Wisconsin. Her four children and third husband, who was about twenty-six years younger than Boyd, buried her in Wisconsin. Four former Union soldiers helped lower the famous Confederate spy into her Northern grave.

Inscribed on her tombstone are the words:

BELLE BOYD

Confederate Spy
Born in Virginia
Died in Wisconsin
Erected by a Comrade

On May 23, 1862 at the Battle of Front Royal, Virginia, Belle Boyd, then eighteen, ran across the battlefield between the firing lines with information for Gen. Stonewall Jackson on the disposition of Union troops. With this information, Jackson broke through and captured Front Royal. Union forces under Gen. Banks were driven from the Shenandoah Valley. "One God. One Flag. One People—Forever." Belle Boyd (Photo by Penny Colman.)

Pauline Cushman also published a book and performed. The book, *Life of Pauline Cushman*, was based on her notes and written by Ferdinand Sarmiento. For her performance, she wore her major's uniform and presented a monologue about her exploits to enthusiastic audiences. Finally she retired from the stage and moved to San Francisco. She lived a meager life and died from an overdose of opium.

An all-male organization of Civil War Veterans, the Grand Army of the Republic (G.A.R.), decided to give Pauline Cushman a full military funeral. The ceremony included thousands of white flowers, flags, an honor guard, and a rifle salute. Cushman was buried in a white coffin in the G.A.R.'s cemetery.

Loreta Janeta Velazquez was another former spy who wrote a book, *The Woman in Battle: A Narrative of the Exploits, Adventures, and Travels of Madame Loreta Janeta Velazquez, Otherwise Known as Lieutenant Harry Buford, Confederate States of America.* After the war, Velazquez headed west. In Omaha, Nebraska,

The back of her headstone is inscribed:
To the Memory of Harriet Tubman Davis
Heroine of the Underground Railroad.
Nurse and Scout in the Civil War.
Born about 1820 in Maryland.
Died March 10, 1913 at Auburn, N.Y.
"Servant of God, Well Done"
Erected by the Empire State Federation of Women's Clubs. July 5, 1937.
(Photo by Penny Colman.)

she talked General W.S. Harney into giving her a revolver, a buffalo robe, and a pair of blankets. Then she traveled to the mining town of Austin, Nevada, where she married a wealthy man and happily settled down.

The final former spy to write a book was Sarah Emma Edmonds. The first edition was called *Nurse and Spy in the Union Army.* Then it was retitled *Unsexed: Or, the Female Soldier.* Two years after the war, Edmonds married a carpenter, Linus Seelye. After their three children died in childhood, they adopted two more, who lived. Edmonds and her family moved around a great deal. Finally they ended up living in La Porte, Texas.

Twenty-three years after the war ended, Sarah Edmonds Seelye applied for a veteran's pension. She wrote to her former comrades and asked for their support. Although they were shocked to discover that she was a woman, they agreed and wrote letters to Congress. Amazingly, Congress voted to "place on the pension roll, the name of Sarah E.E. Seelye, alias Franklin Thompson." For the rest of her life she received a soldier's pension of

$12 per month.

Before her death, Sarah E.E. Seelye became the only woman member of the G.A.R. Like Pauline Cushman, she was buried with a military funeral in a G.A.R. cemetery.

Harriet Tubman also received a government pension, but not because of her heroic service. Instead it was because she was the widow of a Civil War veteran, not because she, too, had served.

General Hunter, General Saxton, and other prominent people tried to get Congress to pay Tubman for her Civil War service. But Congress refused. "It seems strange that one who has done so much for her country and been in the thick of the battles with shots falling all about her, should never have had recognition from the Government ...", a supporter wrote at the time.

That was not the only insult to Tubman's service. On her way home after the war, a white train conductor refused to accept her government pass for half-fare. Then he ordered her to ride in the baggage car. When Tubman refused, the conductor and three white passengers wrestled her into the baggage car. In the struggle, Tubman, who had survived river raids with Colonel Montgomery, suffered an arm and a shoulder injury.

Harriet Tubman lived in Auburn, New York until the age of ninety-three! She, too, was buried with military honors by the G.A.R. A year after her death, the city of Auburn dedicated a plaque to her. The mayor issued a proclamation asking all the citizens to fly their flags on the day the plaque for Tubman was unveiled to "demonstrate that we are not forgetful of those who suffered for the cause of freedom ..."

After the war, Elizabeth Van Lew remained in her mansion. General Sharpe and other supporters tried to get Congress to compensate her for the money she spent to help the Union, but Congress refused.

Fifteen days after he was inaugurated President of the United States, Ulysses Grant appointed Van Lew as

As a final tribute to Elizabeth Van Lew, her Boston admirers shipped a huge hunk of rugged stone to Richmond for her grave. A bronze plaque fastened to the grayish-beige and rose-colored boulder reads: She risked everything that is dear to man—friends, fortune, comfort, health, life itself—all for the one absorbing desire of her heart, that slavery might be abolished and the Union preserved. *(Photo by Penny Colman.)*

post-mistress of Richmond. She kept the position until Rutherford B. Hayes was elected president. Then she was transferred to the post office in Washington, D.C. Ironically, she was forced to resign after a Northern newspaper criticized her transfer.

She returned to Richmond, where she was shunned. "I live and have lived for years as entirely distinct from the citizens as if I were plague stricken," she wrote. When her mother died in 1875, Van Lew wrote, "We had not friends enough to be pall-bearers."

Despite her isolation, Van Lew continued to be a crusader. In particular she adopted the cause of women's suffrage. She never paid her taxes without writing a protest letter, "I do hereby present my solemn protest against the right of any government . . . to levy taxes without representation. I ask that my protest be recorded and published."

For a long time Van Lew lived in great poverty. Finally, she borrowed a stamp and wrote a letter asking for help from the relatives, in Boston, Massachusetts, of one of the officers she had helped in Libby Prison. Without hesitation, they sent her money until her death in 1900.

84

CHRONOLOGY

1861

April 12: Confederate troops open fire on Union troops at Fort Sumter, Charleston, South Carolina.

April 17: Elizabeth Van Lew sees the first Confederate flag flying over Richmond, Virginia.

July 4: Belle Boyd kills a Union soldier in her home in Martinsburg, Virginia (now in West Virginia).

July 10-17: Rose O'Neal Greenhow sends a series of secret messages to warn Confederate troops stationed at Manassas Junction, Virginia, near Bull Run Creek, about Union General McDowell's plan to attack them.

July

21: Forewarned by Greenhow, Confederate troops win the Battle of Bull Run, the first major land battle of the Civil War.

August 23: Rose O'Neal Greenhow is placed under house arrest by Allan Pinkerton in Washington, D.C.

1862

January 18: Greenhow and her daughter are imprisoned in Old Capitol Prison, Washington, D.C.

Early Spring: Harriet Tubman goes to Beaufort, South

Carolina to serve with the Union army as a nurse, scout, and spy.

May 23: Belle Boyd dashes across the battlefield in Front Royal, Virginia, to give important military information to Confederate General Jackson. Confederate troops win the Battle of Front Royal.

June: Rose O'Neal Greenhow and her daughter are released and exiled to Richmond, Virginia.

Late Spring: Sarah Emma Edmonds spies for the Union disguised as a contraband.

July: Congress passes an act that allows free black men to enlist as soldiers.

Nancy Hart is captured by Union soldiers and imprisoned in Summersville, West Virginia. Before long, she kills her jailer and escapes.

On July 25, she returns with 200 Confederate troops and chases the Union troops away.

Belle Boyd is arrested by Union soldiers and imprisoned in Old Capitol Prison, Washington, DC. She is released on August 28th.

1863

Spring: Union spy Pauline Cushman expands her activities and follows Confederate troops through Kentucky and Tennessee. She is arrested and sentenced to be hanged, but is rescued by Union troops the day before she is due to die.

Loreta Velazquez drops her disguise as a male soldier and begins her career as a woman spy.

June 2: Harriet Tubman leads a very successful raid

up the Combahee River in South Carolina.

July 1-3: Confederate troops suffer a staggering defeat at the Battle of Gettysburg.

Late July: Belle Boyd is arrested once again and imprisoned in Carroll Prison, a building connected to Old Capitol Prison in Washington, D.C.

December 2: Belle Boyd is released and exiled to Richmond, Virginia.

1864

May 4: Belle Boyd is arrested once again when the ship she is on is stopped by a Union ship. It is her twentieth birthday. A Union officer, Samuel Hardinge, falls in love with her.

September 30: Rose O'Neal Greenhow dies during an attempt to avoid a Union ship off the coast of Wilmington, North Carolina.

1865

April 3: Union troops capture Richmond, Virginia. Elizabeth Van Lew flies a Union flag from the roof of her mansion.

April 9: Confederate General Robert E. Lee surrenders to Union General Ulysses S. Grant at Appomattox Court House, Virginia. The Union finally wins the Civil War.

April 15: President Abraham Lincoln dies after being shot while attending the theater.

December 18: The Thirteenth Amendment to the Constitution abolishing slavery is ratified.

AFTER THE WAR

1893: Pauline Cushman dies in San Francisco, California.

1897: Loreta Velazquez dies in Austin, Nevada.

1898: Sarah Emma Edmonds dies in La Porte, Texas.

1900: Belle Boyd dies in Kilbourn (now Wisconsin Dells), Wisconsin.

Elizabeth Van Lew dies in Richmond, Virginia.

1902: Nancy Hart dies in Spring Creek, West Virginia.

1913: Harriet Tubman dies in Auburn, New York.

HISTORIC PLACES TO VISIT

BELLE BOYD COTTAGE. 101 Chester Street, Front Royal, Virginia 22630. (703) 636-1446.

BELLE BOYD'S GRAVE. Spring Grove Cemetery, Broadway, Wisconsin Dells, Wisconsin.

HARRIET TUBMAN HOME. 180 South Street, Auburn, New York. (315) 252-2081.

HARRIET TUBMAN'S GRAVE. Fort Hill Cemetery, 19 Fort Street, Auburn, New York.

ROSE O'NEAL GREENHOW'S GRAVE. Oakdale Cemetery, 520 North 15th Street, Wilmington, North Carolina.

ELIZABETH VAN LEW'S GRAVE. Shockoe Hill Cemetery, Hospital Street off First Street, Richmond, Virginia.

FURTHER READING

Bakeless, John. *Spies of the Confederacy*. Philadelphia: J.B. Lippincott Company, 1970.

Beymer, William Gilmore. *On Hazardous Service*. New York: Harper & Brothers, 1912.

Boyd, Belle. *Belle Boyd in Camp and Prison*. Ed. by Curtis Carroll Davis. Cranbury, NJ: Thomas Yoseloff, 1968.

Canon, Jill. *Civil War Heroines*. Santa Barbara, CA: Bellerophon Books, 1991. ✣

Chang, Ina. *A Separate Battle*. New York: Lodestar Books, 1991. (juvenile nonfiction)

Conrad, Earl. *Harriet Tubman*. New York: Paul S. Eriksson, Inc. 1943, 1969.

Dannett, Sylvia G.L., ed. *Noble Women of the North*. New York: Thomas Yoseloff, 1959.

Dannett, Sylvia G.L. *She Rode With the Generals: The True and Incredible Story of Sarah Emma Edmonds Seelye*. New York: T. Nelson, 1960.

Faust, Patricia, ed. *Historical Times Illustrated Encyclopedia of the Civil War*. New York: Harper Perennial, 1986.

Hammond, Harold Earl. *Diary of a Union Lady 1861-1865*. New York: Funk & Wagnalls Company, 1962.

Horan, James D. *Desperate Women*. New York: G.P. Putnam's Sons, 1952.

Jackson, George F. *Black Women Makers of History: A Portrait*. Oakland, CA: GRT Book Printing, 1975. ✻

Jones, Katharine M. *Heroines of Dixie: Confederate Women Tell Their Story of the War*. Indianapolis: The Bobbs-Merrill Company, 1955.

Kane, Harnett T. *Spies for the Blue and Gray*. New York: Hanover House, 1954.

Kinchen, Oscar Aryle. *Women Who Spied for the Blue and Gray*. Philadelphia: Dorrance, 1972.

Meltzer, Milton. *Voices from the Civil War*. New York: Thomas Y. Crowell, 1989. (juvenile nonfiction)

Nolan, Jeannette. *Belle Boyd: Secret Agent*. New York: Messner, 1967. (juvenile fiction)

———. *Spy for the Confederacy: Rose O'Neal Greenhow*. New York: Messner, 1966. (juvenile fiction)

———. *Yankee Spy: Elizabeth Van Lew*. New York: Messner, 1970. (juvenile fiction)

Reit, Seymour. *Beyond Enemy Lines. The Honorable Story of Emma Edmonds*. San Diego: Harcourt, Brace, Jovanovich, 1988. (juvenile fiction)

Ross, Ishbel. *Rebel Rose*. New York: Harper & Brothers, 1954.

Sigaud, Louis A. *Belle Boyd: Confederate Spy*. Richmond: Dietz Press, 1944.

Stern, Philip Van Doren. *Secret Missions of the Civil War*. New York: Rand McNally & Co., 1959.

Tinling, Marion. *Women Remembered: A Guide to*

Landmarks of Women's History in the United States. New York: Greenwood Press, 1986. ✻

Velazquez, Loreta. *The Woman in Battle.* Ed. by C.J. Worthington. New York: Arno Press, 1972.

Woodward, C. Vann. *Mary Chesnut's Civil War.* New Haven, CT: Yale University Press, 1981.

Young, Agatha. *The Women and the Crisis: Women of the North in the Civil War.* New York: McDowell, 1959.

✻ Available from:

National Women's History Project
7738 Bell Road
Windsor, CA 95492
Telephone (707) 838-6000

INDEX